P9-BYN-129

Why Me?

A Spiritual Guide to Growing Through Tests

Life Lessons Gleaned from the Teachings of the Bahá'í Faith

by Justice St Rain

SPECIAL IDEAS

Special Ideas

PO Box 9, Heltonville, IN 47436

1-800-326-1197

Why Me? The Secret of Growing Through Tests

Copyright © 2003 by Justice St Rain

All quotations are from the Sacred Writings of the Bahá'í Faith unless otherwise noted, © National Spiritual Assembly of the United States, used by permission. For references cited, send SASE to above address.

Cover art by Judy Farnsworth.

Cover design by Justice St Rain.

All rights reserved. No part of this book may be reproduced in any form without permission.

First Edition 2003

ISBN #

1-888547-12-X

Printed in the USA

10 9 8 7 6 5 4 3 2 1

03 05 06 07 08 09 10 11 12 13 14

Dedication:

*To Karen,
who moved
my heart from
"Why me?" to
"Thank you!"
on the day we
married.*

Men who suffer not,
attain no perfection.
The plant most pruned by the
gardeners is that one which, when the
summer comes, will have the most beautiful
blossoms and the most abundant fruit.

'Abdu'l-Bahá

Why Me?

O FRIEND!

In the garden of thy heart
plant naught
but the rose of love.

Bahá'u'lláh

Why Me?

When was the last time you asked the universe that question?

When was the last time you stopped and listened for an answer?

Because no matter how rhetorical you thought the question was, there really is an answer—and it is more comforting than you may think.

Of course, like many really important answers, you may not be able to listen to it straight-out. You may have to listen sort of sideways—out of the corner of your ear and between the lines, so to speak—using symbols, metaphor and parable. Parables help your heart listen for the "why" while your mind is absorbed with the "who, what, when and where" stuff.

So I would like to begin this book with a sweet little story called...

The Gardener and the Rose

Once there were four rose bushes in a garden. They spent all summer trying to get each branch to grow as long as possible, and produce as many fragrant blossoms as they could. They were very pleased with their efforts, and were sure that the gardener had noticed their success. So they were all shocked at the end of the summer when the gardener came to each of them with pruning shears and chopped away at their long, beautiful branches.

"Oh my God'ner!" the first one cried. "How could you do such a thing after I worked so long and hard to please you all summer? This is unfair! This is evil! I hate you! I will never do anything you want me to do again!"

"Oh dear, I'm so sorry!" cringed the second rose bush. "I don't know what I did wrong, but I know I must have done something terribly evil to deserve this painful punishment. I promise, I will never do it again!"

The third rose bush was much more philosophical about the experience. "Unfair? Ha! Who said life is fair? Things just happen. Yesterday the gardener watered me, today he chops me to pieces. There is no rhyme or reason behind any of this. You think the gardener knows what he is doing? Shoot— maybe he is drunk, or maybe he takes his orders from someone else. The thing to do is accept your fate and move on."

The fourth rose bush felt the pain of the shears along with the others, but placed it in the context of an entire summer's worth of care and nurturing. She knew that the gardener was not evil, nor was his goal punishment. His actions were neither random nor illogical. The question that she had all winter to consider was, "What does the gardener want me to do or learn in response to this painful experience?"

Months went by, and each rose bush developed a plan of action based on its perceptions of its experience.

In the spring, the first rose bush decided that if the gardener wanted flowers, then it would use its energy to grow roots instead. It explored the dark corners of the garden world, and fed on its compost and manure. But with only a handful of leaves above ground to absorb light and carbon dioxide, the bush soon began to wither and die. Anger and rebellion in the face of suffering did not ease the rose bush's pain.

The second rose bush spent all winter trying to decide what it had done wrong the previous summer to deserve punishment. But the only thing it had done all summer was to grow and blossom. Okay, then, it would not do either of those things. But if a plant does not grow, and a flower does not blossom, then it might as well be dead. Seeing suffering as punishment—and trying to avoid it—did not make the second rose bush any happier or healthier, it only left her paralyzed with inaction.

The third rose bush fared much better. He just did what he had done the year before—sending out a handful of long, scraggly branches with a blossom on the end. Maybe they would get chopped off again, maybe not. It really didn't matter much. Nothing mattered much. So when beetles and aphids began to munch on his leaves and petals, he didn't put up much resistance. They just left that much less for the gardener to come chop off at the end of the summer.

How do you respond when you experience unexpected difficulties?

The fourth rose bush looked at her experience from a different perspective. "Last summer I grew and blossomed. I know that there was nothing wrong with that. The gardener was pleased with me. I trust his judgement, and I trust his actions. So what is it that I am supposed to do differently *this* summer?" she thought to herself. "Well, what I was *planning* on doing was making each of my dozen branches grow another three feet. I wanted to expand on my strengths. But I can't grow out of the end of a cut branch, so how *will* I grow?"

For the first time, the rose bush took a really good look at herself. She was amazed to discover that all along each of her truncated branches there were dozens of tiny nodes—each of which were capable of becoming a whole new branch.

3

Instead of growing a strong bush in twelve ways, she could literally branch out into hundreds of new directions! What a gift the gardener had given her—but only because she was willing to ask the question, "What can I learn from this experience?"

Thinking Like a Rose

Every good parable has a message, and this one is no exception. There are actually three valuable lessons to be learned. First, the rose had to learn to trust the gardener in the face of difficulty. Second, the rose was invited to discover something new about what it means to be a rose bush. Third, learning was only the first step. The rose still had to put forth the extra effort to become the very best rose bush possible.

As humans, we also face tests and difficulties every day. Like the roses, we also have three lessons to learn from them.

First, we are invited to trust the guiding hand of our Creator. No matter how painful or difficult the situation, we will be able to survive and thrive if we have faith in God's love and care.

Second, growth is the result of self-discovery. Unless we know who and what we are, how can we grow? Until we explore our untapped potential, how can we tap it?

Third, growth takes work and commitment. It is easy to wish for an easy life, but it is hard to become the kind of person for whom difficult situations are easy. We have very little control over the things that happen around us, but we have a great deal of control over our willingness and capacity to respond to them.

These are the three lessons of the rose bush. When you really understand them, you can turn a difficult life into a bed of roses.

Trusting the Gardener

If, when we read the story of the rose bushes, we already understand the value of pruning, then we might tend to minimize the strength of faith the fourth rose bush had to exercise. From the rose's perspective, it really did look like the gardener was doing something absolutely awful for no apparent reason.

When absolutely awful things happen to *us* for no apparent reason, most of us find it incredibly difficult to believe that God loves and cares for us. But unless we learn to trust *our* "Gardener," we will be unable to look for the gift behind the pain. Depending on your religious background, this might be very easy or very hard.

Unless we learn to trust our "Gardener," we will be unable to look for the gift behind the pain.

My own religious background is Lutheran-turned-Bahá'í. Because of this, I will be sharing some of the perspectives I have developed by reading the writings of the Bahá'í Faith—as understood through the lens of a fairly standard American Protestant education. Sometimes those two perspectives are in perfect harmony, while other times they clash pretty dramatically. The area of our relationship with God is one of the latter.

The Bahá'í Faith teaches that God is like a loving parent, and that humans are like ignorant children in need of careful guidance. If you grew up in a family or church like mine, in which God was described as an angry, judgmental parent, and humans were seen as sinful creatures deserving of a fiery grave, then you may find it challenging to accept the Bahá'í view.

While I still believe that the Bible is the infallible word of God, I never believed that modern *interpretations* of the Bible were infallible. The popular evangelist Billy Graham, for example, says "God is absolutely pure and holy, and His standard is nothing less than perfection. But no matter how good we are, we can never reach perfection." I can easily agree that God wants us to *strive* for perfection, but for a perfect God to *expect* His imperfect creatures to behave perfectly seems counter to the definition of perfect. We certainly wouldn't say that a *parent* who expected perfection from a child was very wise, and if that parent threatened a child with death for making a mistake, we would call that parent abusive. I can't find it in my heart to imagine that God would feel or act in this way. The error that people make, I believe, is in thinking that perfection is, *of necessity*, intolerant of imperfection. But where is the logic in that? A parent does not expect (or even *want*) a child to be born with the knowledge, maturity and capacity of an adult. Parents love watching the process of growth as it unfolds. So why should a perfect God expect, demand, or even *want* humans to be as perfect as He is?

An excellent dancer loves watching a child's first wobbly steps. An accomplished writer does not criticize a student's first awkward scrawl. An artist does not condemn the colors of an unfinished painting. Nor does a composer damn the chaotic sound of an orchestra in rehearsal. And of course, from our illustration, a gardener will not punish a young rose bush that is only thorns and leaves.

A loving God can be perfect and still love His creation as it struggles for perfection. If you say that the dancer, teacher, artist, etc. are themselves imperfect and are therefore not allowed to condemn imperfection, I must ask "which is more perfect—love or hate?" If we who are imperfect can feel more love than hate for an imperfect effort, then will not God, the Source of perfect love, *also* feel more love than hate, vengeance or anger no matter how imperfect we are?

The Bible says, "God is love." The Bahá'í Writings say that God is "more friend to me than I am to myself." This is the view of God that we must cling to if we ever hope to understand why things happen to us.

God is "more friend to me than I am to myself." This is the view of God that we must cling to.

I say this with such passion because I believe that our expectations concerning our relationship with God will have a huge influence on the way we see tests. If we believe that God is gleefully seeking opportunities to punish us for our mistakes, then we will act like the second rose bush, always expecting punishment and making decisions based on fear rather than love. If we believe that goodness and imperfection are enemies of one another, then we may choose to exaggerate that role like the first rose bush and refuse to do anything we are "supposed" to do as a form of rebellion. As I quipped before, if perfection damns imperfection, we would be right to avoid it—or even resist it.

It is not enough to simply believe that God hates us but forgives us anyway, because this only replaces our fear of punishment with the deadening power of shame. We cannot learn to flourish under God's tender care if our hearts and minds are clouded by feelings of worthlessness and shame.

We must understand that God would not have created us if He hated our imperfections. He knew us and loved us even before He called us into being. When we realize this, then we will be more open to trusting Him and discovering our own true potential. We will be like the fourth rose bush, and look for positive lessons rather than jump to negative conclusions.

"O SON OF MAN! *I loved thy creation, hence I created thee. Wherefore, do thou love Me, that I may name thy name and fill thy soul with the spirit of life.*" —Bahá'u'lláh

The Gift of Tests

So if God loves us so much, how do we make sense of the bad things that happen to us?

Looking at the rose story again, we could say that the first rose bush felt she was being punished for no good reason, so she believed that God was unjust. The second felt that God *was* just, and concluded that she must deserve to be punished. The third decided that the question of justice did not even apply to the situation, and he sought no signs from it. But the fourth decide that the question of *punishment* did not apply to the experience, and looked for the hidden gift.

The idea that tests are *gifts* from God, rather than punishments, is the radical vision that is presented in this book, and it is only available to us if we are willing to trust God and believe in our own essential goodness.

In other words, tests are a source of guidance—they look like punishment, but are really gifts. If we are wise, we will look forward to them so that our spirits will learn how to shine.

I encourage you to set aside your preconceived ideas about tests based on fear, shame and punishment. I invite you to focus instead on *trusting* in God's love and wisdom. Have faith and look for God's hidden gifts.

*"O SON OF MAN!
My calamity is
My providence,
outwardly it is fire
and vengeance,
but inwardly it is
light and mercy.
Hasten thereunto
that thou mayest
become an eternal
light and an
immortal spirit.
This is My command
unto thee, do thou
observe it."*

—*Bahá'u'lláh*

8

Some Background

As I said before, the ideas I am sharing are extensions of the beliefs I've developed as a Bahá'í from a Christian background. Because so much of what I have to say is rooted in that perspective, and it is likely that you, the reader, have had little contact with the Bahá'í Faith before, I want to take a moment here to explain a little bit of the larger Bahá'í context. Here are just a few of the Bahá'í teachings that will make the rest of what I have to say make a little more sense. You don't have to agree with these ideas in order to enjoy this book, but if you *do* agree, then now is a good time to realize it. *(There is more information on the Bahá'í Faith at the end of this book.)*

Bahá'ís are dedicated to:

• *Adoration of One God and the Reconciliation of all Major Religions*

• *Appreciation for the Diversity and Nobility of the Human Family and the Elimination of Prejudice*

• *Establishment of World Peace, Equality of Women and Men, and Universal Education*

• *Cooperation between Science and Religion in the Individual's Search for Truth*

1. Bahá'ís believe that there is only one God; that all the world's major religions come from the same God. So whether you are a Christian, Moslem, Hindu, Buddhist or Jew, Bahá'ís believe in the same God that you do.

2. Bahá'ís believe that our understanding of God matures as we mature—both as individuals and as a society. That is why interpretations that made sense 100 years ago no longer seem logical today.

3. Bahá'ís understand that God is neither male nor female. God is spirit, and we are created in the *spiritual* image of God. For ease of communication, however, I will be referring to God as He throughout this book. If you wish, you may mentally change the word to whatever makes you comfortable.

The Importance of Faith in the Face of Conflicting Evidence

We often think of faith as something we cling to in the absence of facts and evidence. Yet the story of the rose suggests that it is our faith which shapes the facts and evidence of our lives. Consider the first rose bush. She believed that all pain was proof that the world was unfair and unkind. Her response was to hide from the world, focusing her energy on the world below where there *was* no kindness or justice. Her personal experience proved her beliefs to be correct. It was an inescapable negative cycle. Unless she was willing to step outside of her own perspective and consider the other roses' experiences valid, she would return to dust arrogantly certain that the world was an awful place.

> *It is our faith which shapes the facts and evidence of our lives.*

The second rose, too, was blinded by her own beliefs. She believed that pain was a punishment. She believed that she deserved to suffer, so she behaved in a way that filled her life with pain and suffering. This suffering, in turn, proved that she must deserve to be punished. It was a cyclical and therefore inescapable logic.

The third rose bush did not believe in meaning, and so he created for himself a world without meaning, hope or goals. Who could argue against him? He had facts. He had evidence. His life proved that nothing he did made any difference. Anyone who believed differently was an irrational idealist.

Three different rose bushes —three different beliefs—three different worlds. You probably know many people who see the world in each of these ways. Each perspective is absolutely valid and true—as long as it remains isolated from the others. Each is clearly flawed and destructive when viewed from a larger perspective.

This is why faith is so important. This is why the writings of the world's great religions say that we are "saved" by faith.

The fact is that pruning is very helpful to a rose bush. It is a gift, a blessing—a means of its growth and perfection. But there is no way to recognize, demonstrate or experience this fact unless you first have enough faith in the gardener to let him cut your prized plant.

Likewise, pain, suffering, tests and difficulties are all very helpful for the human soul. They help us grow. But it is very difficult to experience this growth if our minds tell us that they are accidents, our hearts tell us they are punishments, and the whole world tells us that we should avoid them at all costs because they are evil and destructive.

Once we are blessed with faith, then our behavior changes. New behavior produces new experiences. New experiences open our eyes to a whole new world of understanding.

We must have faith. Once we are blessed with faith, then our behavior changes. New behavior produces new experiences. New experiences open our eyes to a whole new world of under-standing—the world of the fourth rose bush.

This fourth world is the real world.

How do I know that?

If each world-view is internally consistent, then how do we know which one is "real?" We know because the *real* one is big enough to contain all the others, but the imagined ones only exist within themselves.

In the real world, the Gardener gives us exactly what we need in order to grow and develop, but He gives us the choice of how to respond. This view explains what happened to each of the four rose bushes.

False world-views are good at justifying pain and suffering, but they aren't very good at explaining joy, growth or transformation. Believing that the gardener was evil may explain what happened to the first rose bush, but why would an evil gardener do something that would help the fourth bush grow and develop? Likewise, what kind of punishment would it be to help a rose discover its full potential? Many people see the world as a series of random accidents with no meaning or purpose, but what drunk gardener would "accidentally" prune a bush just enough to let it grow twice as big the next year?

When we witness radiant souls who transform stumbling blocks into stepping stones and trials into triumphs, then we cannot deny the evidence that each of us has the capacity to do the same.

This faith, then, even if it is initially based on the facts and efforts of other people's lives, gives us the perspective we need to transform our own failures into opportunities for growth. When we see our tests as gifts from God, then that is exactly what they will become. We will then have our own facts and experiences to prove the goodness of God and the value of tests. When this time comes, we will probably not even think of it as *faith*, but will consider it *wisdom*.

So if we tentatively decide to trust God, and believe that whatever He allows to happen to us must be a gift, then what? Like the rose, trusting the Gardener was only one third of the process. The second step comes from understanding yourself, and the third is expressed in action and growth.

Discovering Your True Nature

What does it mean to be a human? What hidden qualities do we have that we haven't discovered yet? Why are we here? How do we become the very best people we can be? These are the questions that tests and difficulties invite us to explore. But if we completely misunderstand the answer to the first question—What is a human?—Then we can never find useful answers to the other three.

If a rose bush had never seen another rose bush and was planted in a field of potatoes, then it might think it was a potato, and like our first rose bush, put a lot of energy into developing a root system that did it little good. If humans look around at the world of nature and decide that they are animals without souls, then they will imitate animals, and never develop the special capacities that are like the blossoms of the human spirit. It is true that both a rose and a potato have roots, and both humans and animals have bodies, but it is what we develop above the *earth*ly plane that makes the difference.

Spiritual Beings with a Spiritual Purpose

Bahá'ís believe that we are noble spirits, created in the image of God, and given the capacities of knowledge, understanding, self-awareness and growth.

O SON OF SPIRIT! I created thee rich, why dost thou bring thyself down to poverty? Noble I made thee, wherewith dost thou abase thyself? Out of the essence of knowledge I gave thee being,

*why seekest thou enlightenment from anyone beside Me? Out of
the clay of love I molded thee, how dost thou busy thyself with
another? Turn thy sight unto thyself, that thou mayest find Me
standing within thee, mighty, powerful and self-subsisting.*

Bahá'u'lláh

*O SON OF MAN!
Veiled in My
immemorial being
and in the ancient
eternity of My
essence, I knew My
love for thee; therefore
I created thee, have
engraved on thee
Mine image and
revealed to thee
My beauty.
—Bahá'u'lláh*

Out of these capacities blossom a
host of God-like virtues such as love,
patience, wisdom, honesty, justice, courage, and compassion. These virtues are
expressions of our very essence and reflect our true spiritual nature.

As spirits, we are eternal and immortal. We are creatures *made in the image
of God*. This does not mean that we *are*
God. It means that we reflect the image of God in the same way as a mirror
reflects the light of the sun.

We know that the sun sends its light
into every corner of the universe. Only a
few of its rays ever land on earth, and
only a handful of them can be reflected in any one mirror. Yet
each mirror that is clean and polished, and turns its surface to
the sky can capture the image of the sun's globe and reflect its
warmth and illumination.

It is God's virtues that are reflected in the human heart,
and because each of us has the capacity to reflect those virtues,
we are told that we are made in the image of God.

This is the reason we were created—to receive the light of
God's love and reflect His qualities. To help us do that, God
gave us bodies and placed us in the material world where we
encounter tests, difficulties and many unique learning experiences. These experiences "polish" our souls so that we can
reflect divine virtues more perfectly.

This material world is designed to help us develop our individuality and grow spiritually in the same way as our mother's womb is designed to protect and nourish us while we develop physically.

The vision of our human souls reflecting the qualities of God is a beautiful, uplifting and inspiring one. It is also very complex and profound, with many implications for our daily lives. In order to more fully understand the concept of reflecting God's qualities, it is helpful to break it down into three distinct but inseparable parts:

Knowing and Loving God,

Developing Virtues and

Carrying Forward an Ever-Advancing Civilization.

These can be seen as mystical, personal and social aspects of the same idea. Or you can think of them as three relationships. We have a relationship with God—the source of the qualities we are trying to reflect. We have a relationship with ourselves—perfecting our ability to reflect. And we have a relationship with the world—the place where we shine our reflected light.

Bahá'ís believe that to know God is to know the qualities and virtues of God, such as kindness, justice, wisdom, creativity, etc. To love those qualities is to want to reflect them in our own behavior, that is, to develop those virtues personally. This requires us to know ourselves very well and to acknowledge our ability to shine. When we develop these qualities and express them in our relationships with others, then civilization as a whole advances. These three interconnected concepts are presented very nicely in the following three quotations:

To know God is to know the qualities and virtues of God, such as kindness, justice, wisdom, creativity, etc.

15

Having created the world and all that liveth and moveth therein, He, through the direct operation of His unconstrained and sovereign Will, chose to confer upon man the unique distinction and capacity to know Him and to love Him—a capacity that must needs be regarded as the generating impulse and the primary purpose underlying the whole of creation.... Upon the inmost reality of each and every created thing He hath shed the light of one of His names, and made it a recipient of the glory of one of His attributes. Upon the reality of man, however, He hath focused the radiance of all of His names and attributes, and made it a mirror of His own Self. Alone of all created things man hath been singled out for so great a favor, so enduring a bounty.

Bahá'u'lláh

The first, the fundamental purpose underlying creation hath ever been, and will continue to be, none other than the appearance of trustworthiness and godliness, of sincerity and goodwill amongst mankind, for these qualities are the cause of peace, security and tranquillity. Blessed are those who possess such virtues.

Bahá'u'lláh

> **"All men have been created to carry forward an ever-advancing civilization."**
>
> **—Bahá'u'lláh**

All men have been created to carry forward an ever-advancing civilization. The Almighty beareth Me witness: To act like the beasts of the field is unworthy of man. Those virtues that befit his dignity are forbearance, mercy, compassion and loving-kindness towards all the peoples and kindreds of the earth.

Bahá'u'lláh

16

Practicing Virtues

So if we are spiritual beings trying to reflect the qualities of God in a material world, where do tests fit in? The key word in this explanation of the human condition is the word "trying." Sometimes when we try something we succeed. Then we are happy with ourselves and are pleased that we have had an opportunity to learn and grow. Sometimes when we try we fail. When this happens, we often feel bad, get upset, and even look around for someone or something to blame. The more important the activity, the more serious it is when we fail. If we "try" to find a parking place and fail, then we can get pretty upset, but if we "try" to drive to work and fail (by driving off the road, for example) then we become painfully aware that we are in the middle of a test.

Most of us over the age of 18 do not think of driving a car as a test of our capacities. We are not even really aware that we are "trying" to do something difficult—but we are. Just ask a 15-year-old trying to learn how to merge onto an interstate at 60 m.p.h. When he or she contemplates taking the state driver's test, it *really is a test.*

We are each born with the capacity to reflect and develop an infinite array of divine qualities and virtues.

The point is that a situation is only a test if it is new enough to seem difficult. Once an activity becomes a habit, it is second nature to us. It is no longer a test. Tests and difficulties are themselves the means by which we are transformed from nervous newcomers to confident performers.

Now consider the fact that we are each born with the capacity to reflect and develop an infinite array of divine qualities and virtues. Each one of those virtues takes practice; each quality requires effort.

These spiritual capacities are the essence of who we are, and yet they come to us in stages. Like a tiny seed, we each contain within ourselves the potential for every human perfection. Like a baby rose bush, each of our spiritual "stems" is capable of growing in dozens of new directions, but it requires time, energy, and yes, even a little pruning in order to "branch out."

Imagine yourself for a moment, confident and calm, at peace with yourself and your family. Unruffled by the chaos at work, patient and tolerant in your interactions with your children, generous with friends, sympathetic with strangers, incredibly perceptive and creative when faced with new situations, wise beyond your years....

And all of these qualities are within you. They can each become "second nature" just like driving a car or walking and chewing gum at the same time. But they take practice.

Each time we practice one of these spiritual qualities, we run the risk of failure. Each time we practice one of these qualities, we run the risk of failure. But both failure and success teach us something new about ourselves. Each time we "try out" a new virtue or capacity, we move closer to our full potential. We become more true to ourselves and reflect a little more of God's light. The test itself helps us grow, whether we pass it or not.

From this perspective, we should all be looking forward to tests, right? We all want to grow. We all want to practice being our true selves. We all want to exercise our full capacities, right? But it doesn't usually work that way.

Why not? Well, one of the big problems is that we can't exercise a virtue that we don't know we have. We all have parts of our character that we recognize as "me"—qualities that we feel comfortable practicing with confidence. But our capacities are infinite. There are all sorts of talents and virtues that we don't even know exist until we find ourselves in a situation where we need them.

Consider the rose bush. She loved the part of her that could grow long skinny branches with a flower on the end. It was beautiful. Why should she ever want to grow any differently? But when she lost the ability to grow long, she discovered the ability to grow wide. This test was a gift from the gardener, but her response to it was her gift to herself.

When we get caught up in the material world around us, it is easy to remain unaware of our *spiritual* capacities. When we forget about our spiritual capacities, then it is up to God to remind us of them.

Born with an infinite array of virtues, we need to experience an infinite variety of opportunities to practice them.

Born with an infinite array of virtues, we need to experience an infinite variety of opportunities to practice them. While some of these opportunities will be created by our own behavior, others will be provided by God. In either case, it is up to *us* to turn the opportunity into a gift rather than into a punishment.

When my first marriage crashed and burned, it was hard for me to see it as a gift. When I went bankrupt a few months later, I could only see it as a source of shame. Then when the IRS came after me, I had had enough. What was God trying to do to me, anyway?

But when I looked at these three tests together, all hitting within a short period of time, I realized that they represented my three biggest fears in life—failure with love, failure with money and failure in my relationship with authority.

These failures confirmed for me my most deeply rooted beliefs about myself.

If I wanted to pass these tests, I would have to change these beliefs. And I *did* want to pass these tests. I didn't have much choice. They were too big for my previous coping skills of running, hiding or denying to deal with.

So I looked deep inside and found the spiritual qualities that I needed in order to succeed—qualities that I had been told all of my life did not exist within me. I had been told that I was a rogue—wild, irresponsible and rebellious, so of course my life was destined to come unraveled. But upon closer in-spection, I realized that it was my *iden-tity*, not my life, that required reweaving. Maturity, responsibility, integrity and commitment were all hiding behind a sackcloth of low expectations, but they were there all along. After ten years of sunlight and exercise they are now a con-scious part of who I am and how I see myself. Even more important, I now realize that they are how *God* sees me.

When we test our spiritual qualities, we don't just use them, we become them.

What a gift.

So, in retrospect, was the gift of learning something about my true self worth the many years of suffering I went through?

Yep.

When we test our spiritual qualities, we don't just use them, we *become them*. And that is the only way to be truly alive.

The more difficulties one sees in the world the more perfect one becomes. The more you plough and dig the ground the more fertile it becomes. The more you put the gold in the fire the purer it becomes. The more you sharpen the steel by grinding the better it cuts. Therefore, the more sorrows one sees the more perfect one becomes. That is why, in all times, the Prophets of God have had tribulations and difficulties to withstand. The more often the captain of a ship is in the tempest and difficult sailing the greater his knowledge becomes. Therefore I am happy that you have had great tribulations and difficulties. For this I am very happy—that you have had many sorrows. Strange it is that I love you and still I am happy that you have sorrows.

'Abdu'l-Bahá

"Strange it is that I love you and still I am happy that you have sorrows."

Section Summary:

The purpose of our lives is to develop virtues. Tests can be seen as opportunities to practice these virtues. When we do not actively seek these opportunities, then God brings them to us. These tests are the tools God uses to help us learn how to reflect His qualities.

Tests that Are Gifts from God

Once we understand that tests are really opportunities to grow, we can ask ourselves three important questions about each test we face: First, what is the source of this test? Is it a gift from God, or is it the result of our own behavior? Second, what will our attitude be towards this test? Will we approach it as an opportunity for growth and learn from it, or will we consider it a punishment and try to avoid it? Finally, what virtue or capacity might the situation be exercising? The sooner and more accurately we can identify an area of growth potential, the better we can nurture its development.

We will start by looking at the tests that come from God, and try to understand the wide range of purposes they serve. In doing this, we will explore both tests that we accept as opportunities, and those we rebel against and experience as punishment. These are the first two kinds of tests.

We will explore both tests that we accept as opportunities, and those we rebel against.

These tests...do but cleanse the spotting of self from off the mirror of the heart, till the Sun of Truth can cast its rays thereon....
'Abdu'l-Bahá

You've heard the slogan *"no pain, no gain."* We accept this idea without question when applied to the strengthening of our physical potential. Why should developing our spiritual strengths be any different? If our muscles ache after a game of baseball, we don't fall into a depression thinking the coach was trying to punish us. We recognize that we must have stretched some muscles we hadn't used in a while. The same thing happens when we are called upon to be more patient, tolerant, forgiving or generous than we are used to. It makes us stretch, and that can hurt.

What at first sounds like a shallow, naive explanation actually contains within it an inescapable logic. Suppose, for example, that God desires for you the gift of patience. The first thing to do would be to put you in a very long line at the grocery store so that you could practice being patient. The ironic thing is that if you passed this test easily, you wouldn't even know it was a test because you wouldn't be feeling impatient!

I heard a Bahá'í speaker illustrate this point humorously when he asked members of an audience to raise their hands if they wanted to become more forgiving. When everyone's hand was raised, he asked how many wanted a friend to do something mean to them so that they would have something to forgive. All hands dropped!

Every single virtue—love, patience, wisdom, courage, honesty—takes practice to develop. Practice involves failure, and it is our failures—great, small, and unavoidable—that we perceive as tests. On the other hand, practice ultimately assures success, so this same practice can be perceived as opportunity.

The Bahá'í Writings offer this insight:

Thou didst write of afflictive tests that have assailed thee. To the loyal soul, a test is but God's grace and favour; for the valiant doth joyously press forward to furious battle on the field of anguish, when the coward, whimpering with fright, will tremble and shake. So too, the proficient student, who hath with great competence mastered his subjects and committed them to memory, will happily exhibit his skills before his examiners on the day of his tests. So too will solid gold wondrously gleam and shine out in the assayer's fire.

It is clear, then, that tests and trials are, for sanctified souls, but God's bounty and grace, while to the weak, they are a calamity, unexpected and sudden.   'Abdu'l-Bahá

Because I was a good student, I really identify with the image of actually enjoying tests when I knew I would pass them easily. I was that obnoxious kid waving his hand whenever the teacher asked a question. For some of you, however, another image might work better. For me, trying to hit a baseball was a humiliating test that I failed continuously. I really did think the coach was out to get me. For my friends, however, the chance to play ball was not a test, but a pleasure. They clamored to be next at bat while I tried to be invisible. They had confidence in their ability, while I did not.

Likewise, each of us has spiritual strengths and weaknesses that will seem amazing or ridiculous to people around us. It doesn't matter. Our tests are OUR gifts from God, and struggling with them brings nobility and confirmations to our lives.

Men who suffer not, attain no perfection. The plant most pruned by the gardeners is that one which, when the summer comes, will have the most beautiful blossoms and the most abundant fruit.

The labourer cuts up the earth with his plough, and from that earth comes the rich and plentiful harvest. The more a man is chastened, the greater is the harvest of spiritual virtues shown forth by him. A soldier is no good General until he has been in the front of the fiercest battle and has received the deepest wounds.
'Abdu'l-Bahá

We have all been wounded by life. Fortunately we are not judged by our wounds but by our willingness to learn from them and move forward. It is our response to tests, not the tests themselves, that strengthens our virtues.

Being Receptive to Tests

Just as we choose how we respond to tests, God chooses which tests to give us based on our maturity and receptivity.

Know thou that ordeals are of two kinds: One is for tests, and the other for punishment of misdeeds. That which is for testing is for one's education and development, and that which is for punishment of deeds is severe retribution.

The father and the teacher sometimes show tenderness towards the children and at other times deal harshly with them. Such severity is for educational purposes; it is true tenderness and absolute bounty and grace. Although in appearance it is wrath, in reality it is kindness. Although outwardly it is an ordeal, inwardly it is cooling draught.

In both cases prayers and supplications should be offered at the sacred Threshold, so that thou mayest remain firm in tests, and patient in ordeals.   'Abdu'l-Bahá

Since many of us have had harsh teachers, it may be hard to imagine a loving teacher acting in a way that feels callous, but isn't. Lets explore how the methods used for teaching might depend on our spiritual receptivity.

Using my experience in both the classroom and the playing field as analogies, we can imagine that when a person is just beginning to learn a skill, they must be motivated to make an effort. This is true whether it is learning to read or learning to hit a ball. If a person is easily motivated to do his or her best, then tests are a welcome opportunity for practice, but if motivation is lacking, tests will always be perceived as a punishment. If the threat of a test motivates a student to perfect a skill, it is likely he or she will eventually begin to enjoy the activity. Later, tests can be used to determine which areas need more practice and to demonstrate improvement.

As skills are mastered, tests provide opportunities for success and celebration, and finally, tests can take place in a way that allows others to learn from the success or failure.

This list describes the positive progression that we can choose in responding to tests:

- **Become motivated**
- **Demonstrate mastery**
- **Identify weaknesses**
- **Become a living example**

Receptive souls take this path to wisdom, virtue and a more joyful relationship with God. We will look at these steps a little more closely in the next few pages.

On the other hand, some choose a more negative path. If all efforts at encouragement and motivation fail, then there are natural consequences. The skills that a teacher or coach are trying to teach may not look important, but they usually are. Each refusal to practice, each failure to develop a skill, makes it more and more difficult to participate in the goal activity. At some point, those who cannot or will not participate must be removed from the activity. This is a natural consequence, and may not even seem like a punishment to those who did not wish to participate in the first place. No teacher or coach wants this, and neither does God, but it is no more possible to make people want to develop spiritual qualities than it is to make them enjoy learning or playing ball. We each have a choice.

- **Avoidance/Denial**
- **Anger/Belligerence**
- **Rejection/Refusal**
- **Expulsion/Removal**

This is the negative progression that we can choose in responding to tests, and is, unfortunately, the one we usually think of when things happen that we don't like. Fortunately, by having confidence in our capacity and choosing to be receptive, we are more likely to pass our tests quickly and with less anxiety.

Tests That Motivate

In the previous section, I described a range of tests that are reflective of our maturity and receptivity. The first of these are tests that motivate us to want to improve by helping us see the advantages of developing our virtues.

O friends! Be not careless of the virtues with which ye have been endowed, neither be neglectful of your high destiny.

Bahá'u'lláh

It seems to me that most people are not evil or mean or even selfish. We are simply careless.

What I mean is, we are careless with our virtues. It is as though we were given a box of precious gems, and we leave them spilled across the kitchen table where they get dribbled on, knocked off and buried under last week's mail. We forget who we are. We forget why we are here. We forget our high destiny, and we forget the value of what we were given.

So now and then, we look up from our lasagna and realize that we've buried our honesty and lost our patience, tripped over our grace, and landed in the middle of a heap of trouble.

That's when we start begging God for help—and that's when we start remembering that God gave us all of the honesty, patience and grace that we need if we just weren't so careless!

So we start to care *more.*

We start to care about our virtues. We start to polish them— even when they aren't on display. We start to enjoy the way they sparkle and shine when the rest of the world is so dark. We start to actually enjoy being good. We enjoy being able to remain serene while the clerk fumbles while changing the cash register tape. We feel a happy buzz as we return the twenty dollar bill that the person in front of us drops without noticing, and our hearts soar as we practice random acts of kindness.

If we can hold onto these sensations, we can avoid some of the most painful and confusing of all of God's tests. But how many of us will? How many of us remember to want to be spiritual every day of our lives? Not many.

While a man is happy he may forget his God; but when grief comes and sorrows overwhelm him, then will he remember his Father who is in Heaven, and who is able to deliver him from his humiliations.   'Abdu'l-Bahá

Even when we desire spirituality in general, we may forget the value of a particular virtue, so we will all continue to get motivational tests. The question is—how bad do they have to be and for how long before we remember to turn to God for help and find His strength within us?

I have my own personal way of dividing tests. Some I experience as "gentle nudges" and others I call "baseball bat to the head" tests. My goal is to be aware of the nudges, but there have been several times in my life in which I had to be "flattened" in order to notice that I was not exercising an important virtue. I know I am not alone. The people of the world have lived through countless sorrows, both individually and collectively in the last few generations, and yet we keep moving away from God and our own "high destiny."

How many of our current personal and social problems could be solved quickly and easily by the application of a few of the simple virtues that we have carelessly (and irreverently) tossed aside? Love, patience, compassion, generosity, chastity and faith—I think these could handle almost anything.

Tests That Identify
Strengths and Weaknesses

The Kingdom of God is possessed of limitless potency. Auda-cious must be the army of life if the confirming aid of that King-dom is to be repeatedly vouchsafed unto it....Vast is the arena, and the time ripe to spur on the charger within it. Now is the time to reveal the force of one's strength, the stoutness of one's heart and the might of one's soul.   'Abdu'l-Bahá

There is a difference between thinking of tests as a way of identifying strengths and weaknesses and thinking of them as ways to sort people between winners and losers, smart and stupid, good and bad. This sorting process is how we usually experienced tests in school—from reading tests that put us in the "fast" or "slow" reading group in first grade to the SAT that determined which college we could attend. But God is a more loving and patient teacher than most of us are used to.

Imagine for a moment a coach for a big city high school with 200 boys wanting to play on the baseball team. When this coach ran drills and tests, it would be for the purpose of crossing kids off the list as quickly as possible so he could find a dozen or so superstars for the school team.

Now imagine a coach for a tiny school with only two dozen students—boys and girls combined. This coach would also run drills and give tests, but the goal would be entirely different. The goal would be to identify each individual's strengths and weaknesses so that they could be balanced and developed as part of a unified whole. Each and every student would be important. Every strength would be utilized, and every weak-ness compensated for.

Or imagine a medical school in Africa during a famine. Teachers would do everything in their power to help students pass their tests so that more doctors would be trained to treat the needy. Each student would be valued because each newly trained doctor could save hundreds of lives.

> *God is not interested in crossing us off of lists. Each of us is infinitely important.*

God is not interested in crossing us off of lists. Each of us is infinitely important.

Do you believe that? Many don't. Most of us have grown up being sorted and shuffled. We looked around and saw that there were millions of people in the world taking the same tests and doing the same work, and we came to believe that, surely, God had crossed us off of His list in His search for a spiritual superstar.

But the work before us does not require superstars. It requires the coordination, balance and teamwork that come from understanding our strengths and weaknesses.

The problem with thinking of tests as a way of sorting people is that it encourages us to give up on ourselves. In school, the kids in the slow reading group were allowed to fall farther and farther behind. The kids that didn't make first string in sports were left sitting on the bench all year. Our whole social system is organized around the idea that "some people got it and some don't." But when it comes to spiritual qualities, we've all "got it."

We are each born with the capacity to reflect the qualities of God. Just because we are not doing a good job of it today does not mean that God is going to check us off His list and give up on us. What He *will* do is give us a test that points out where we need to grow and invite us to respond accordingly.

If we think that the test is designed to eliminate us from the game, then we are more likely to ignore, deny or hide our mistakes instead of learning from them.

If we think tests are a way of sorting people, we may allow one mistake to define us—insisting that it reflects our true nature—something we can't change. We may lose confidence in our ability to succeed, and give up on ourselves.

But God knows that our strengths and weaknesses are not carved in stone. He will not "flunk" us the first time we take a test. He will give us dozens, if not thousands of opportunities to develop each of our virtues. It is easy for God to forgive our mistakes and give us another chance to learn. It is harder for us to do the same.

God knows that our strengths and weaknesses are not carved in stone.

Forgiveness can be particularly difficult when we notice that today we failed a test that we passed last week. Virtues must become habits, and habits are developed through repeated practice, so it is only natural that there is a "spiritual learning curve" involved. Once we recognize a lesson, we are usually well on our way to learning it, but we are not necessarily proficient, so we must be patient with ourselves when we "backslide" in our efforts.

When we finally reach the "plateau" of spiritual proficiency in one area, then the tests do not necessarily stop, but their character changes. They become less of a *test* of our capacities, and more of a *demonstration*, or even *celebration* of them.

But why would God continue to test us after we have learned a lesson? Well, there are two good reasons. First is the simple fact that we are developing our virtues because they are useful. They aren't trophies to be set on a shelf; they are tools to be utilized in service.

The second is that we often forget to use the capacities that we already have to their fullest potential. Tests give us the chance to "flex our spiritual muscles," so to speak. They give us a chance to explore "the might of our soul," and to rise above our own expectations. We come to realize that we are capable of more than we think.

We often forget to use the capacities that we already have to their fullest potential.

The Bahá'í Writings are full of quotations that talk about using tests to separate the true from the false, the gold from the dross, the brave from the coward. It is tempting, based on our past experience, to think of these quotations as proof that God is trying to sort us out—to find the failures and send them off to hell. But I would like for you to consider them from a different perspective. I would like for you to think of them from the perspective of someone who has passed the test, and now sees for the first time his or her true potential. It is a glorious feeling.

You see, God already knows our strengths and weaknesses. He has no need or desire to sort us into "goats and sheep." It is *we* who need to understand who we are and how we need to grow. When we fail a test, then we learn something important. These are spiritual life skills we are talking about, and we need to know if they are lacking.

But when we pass a test, we learn something equally important. We discover a strength within ourselves that we didn't know existed. We begin to glow with a new inner light. We gain a confidence that will allow us to face new challenges.

So I invite you to read these quotations as one who has accepted the challenge of passing the test. You can, you know. You can gleam like gold in the fire of tests, and acquire a luster that will not tarnish.

Not until man is tried doth the pure gold distinctly separate from the dross. Torment is the fire of test wherein the pure gold shineth resplendently and the impurity is burned and blackened.

'Abdu'l-Bahá

Were it not for tests, pure gold could not be distinguished from the impure. Were it not for tests, the courageous could not be separated from the cowardly. Were it not for tests, the people of faithfulness could not be known from the disloyal. Were it not for tests, the intellectuals and the faculties of the scholars in great colleges would not develop. Were it not for tests, sparkling gems could not be known from worthless pebbles. Were it not for tests, nothing would progress in this contingent world.

'Abdu'l-Bahá

Anybody can be happy in the state of comfort, ease, health, success, pleasure and joy; but if one will be happy and contented in the time of trouble, hardship and prevailing disease, it is the proof of nobility.

'Abdu'l-Bahá

Tests Experienced As Punishments

Earlier I said that tests were defined, in part, by our response to them. What kind of response turns an opportunity into a punishment? In the previous section, I described the positive path of tests from God—from motivation to growth to celebration and opportunity. Because we have free will, we each also have the ability to follow the opposite path. We can resist motivation, rebel against growth, and reap the pain that comes from spiritual emptiness. God is the same loving Creator. The tests are the same open doors, but the soul has taken a different path and suffers the consequences.

We are never given a test that we cannot pass, but we are often given tests that we will not pass.

Just as God knows that we are able to pass a test, He also knows when we will choose to refuse. We are never given a test that we cannot pass, but we are often given tests that we *will not* pass. From one perspective, this could be the definition of punishment. With absolute justice, God continues to offer us opportunities for growth—knowing in advance that we will refuse them, and that our refusal may cause us pain.

It would be unjust for God to withhold opportunities for our growth, because spiritual growth is more important than avoiding pain. That is why the Sacred Writings of all religions tell us that it is wise to fear God's justice.

The Fear of the Lord is the beginning of wisdom.

Proverbs

The essence of wisdom is the fear of God, the dread of His scourge and punishment, and the apprehension of His justice and decree.

Bahá'u'lláh

34

In explaining the fear of God to children,....the child should be made to understand that we don't fear God because He is cruel, but we fear Him because He is just, and, if we do wrong and deserve to be punished, then in His justice He may see fit to punish us. We must both love God and fear Him.

Shoghi Effendi

Justice hath a mighty force at its command. It is none other than reward and punishment for the deeds of men. By the power of this force the tabernacle of order is established throughout the world, causing the wicked to restrain their natures for fear of punishment.

Bahá'u'lláh

Should we disobey God and work against His commands He will view our acts in the light of justice and punish us for it. That punishment may not be in the form of fire, as some believe, but in the form of spiritual deprivation and degradation.

Shoghi Effendi

After all of these quotations about fear and punishment, it is important to explain the distinction between "educational punishment" and vengeful punishment. When a parent says "eat your broccoli, or you won't get to watch TV tonight," that is educational punishment. Eating broccoli is a good thing that a child perceives as bad, while not watching TV will cause no harm, but is perceived as even worse than eating broccoli. No harm is intended, and no real harm is done. This kind of punishment is a kindness.

It is important to understand the distinction between "educational punishment" and vengeful punishment.

Vengeful punishment is when there is a desire to repay disobedience with hurt. "Eat your broccoli or I will beat the livin' tar out of you!" This is the kind of punishment that some people have intimate experience with, and the kind that can make us fear sources of authority—including God. But God does not engage in this kind of punishment. You will remember that even as Christ was nailed to the cross, He said *"Father forgive them, for they know not what they do."* This is the example of forgiveness that we can all rely on.

You can see that Bahá'ís are not big on "fire and brimstone," but we do believe that God's "educational punishment" can be expressed in some very unexpected ways. There is a famous saying that goes, "When God wants to punish us He answers our prayers." There is an interesting logic behind that perspective.

What greater punishment can we imagine than to be spiritually empty and forget who we really are?

If a parent allows a willful child to eat an entire gallon of ice cream, the bellyache of an over-stuffed stomach will be an appropriate punishment. Likewise, if God allows a selfish person to distract themselves with money and possessions, then the heartache of an empty soul will be its own punishment. Indeed, what greater punishment can we imagine than to be spiritually empty and forget who we really are?

Indeed shouldst Thou desire to confer blessing upon a servant Thou wouldst blot out from the realm of his heart every mention or disposition except Thine Own mention; and shouldst Thou ordain evil for a servant by reason of that which his hands have unjustly wrought before Thy face, Thou wouldst test him with the benefits of this world and of the next that he might become preoccupied therewith and forget Thy remembrance.

The Báb

You might wonder if there were any times when God's punishment might go beyond our mere perception—when God really did want us to suffer?

36

Could we do something so bad that God would not for-give us? Would God ever do something so horrible to us that there was no possible way to turn it into a growth experience? No.

...Thou art the Generous, and verily Thou art the All-Merci-ful, and verily Thou art the Ever-Forgiving, He to Whom repen-tance is due, He Who forgiveth even the most grievous of sins.

'Abdu'l-Bahá

When it comes down to the essence of life, the only thing of any value to us in the universe, and I mean the ONLY thing of value to us in the entire UNIVERSE, is our own capacity to reflect the virtues of God within our hearts. These virtues are the essence of our true reality and without them we are noth-ing. Once God has given us the capacity to manifest His quali-ties, the only source of harm, pain or punishment in the entire universe is our own free will capacity to ignore those virtues and remain empty. In other words, *we* are the only ones who can punish ourselves.

Unfortunately, we are very good at it.

O SON OF MAN! Sorrow not save that thou art far from Us. Rejoice not save that thou art drawing near and returning unto Us. Bahá'u'lláh

"And be ye not like those who forget God, and whom He hath therefore caused to forget their own selves." Bahá'u'lláh

True loss is for him whose days have been spent in utter igno-rance of his self. Bahá'u'lláh

O SON OF BEING! Love Me, that I may love thee. If thou lovest Me not, My love can in no wise reach thee. Know this, O servant. Bahá'u'lláh

A Bahá'í friend once asked me, "But what about the firing squad of 750 soldiers who shot The Báb, (the first of the two Bahá'í Prophets)? They were all killed by an earthquake or executed within three years. Wasn't that a vengeful punishment?"

Certainly many Bahá'ís believe that this was a sign of God's vengeance, but I don't—not because I don't believe that God was involved, but because I believe that God is beyond vengeance as a motive. So how can I maintain that killing 750 people is not, of necessity, a punishment?

This is a very powerful question—with a very subtle answer. What I am suggesting will only make sense to you if you look at it from a spiritual perspective. If we consider death a punishment, then God punishes saints and sinners alike. But Bahá'ís see death as a transition into the spiritual world—certainly not a punishment. I have known many spiritual people of all religions who are sincerely looking forward to death.

The 750 soldiers who died entered the realm of the spirit. Whether they consider that a blessing or a punishment is up to them. If they were attached to the physical world, then they may be unhappy. If they had not developed their virtues, then they might be helpless. If they realized that they had played a part in the martyrdom of a Prophet of God, then they may spend eternity overwhelmed by remorse and shame. But if they were good, loving people who sincerely believed that they were doing the Will of God, and asked forgiveness when they realized that they were wrong, then I believe that God forgave them and they are progressing spiritually.

> *"Vengeance is mine;*
> *I will repay,*
> *saith the Lord."*
> *Romans 12:19*

So why do the writings of all of the world's religions talk so much about God's wrath and punishment?

You have to look at it from a developmental standpoint. The Bahá'í Faith teaches that throughout history, God has always spoken to us in the language that was appropriate for the time. Like a good parent who uses different forms of discipline for children of different ages, God also motivates us with the rewards and punishments that we will understand.

A spiritual person is not afraid of death, but a materially-oriented person is. When God allows 750 people to die after shooting a Prophet, it is not necessarily seen as a punishment for the people who step into the spiritual realm, but it *is* seen as a punishment by the materially-minded people who are left behind. This "punishment" is then a source of motivation and education for generations to come.

The idea that punishment is relative may be difficult to accept when we are looking at the extreme of death, so lets look at another analogy. Imagine a friend and me in gym class playing baseball. He loves sports, I hate them, but we are in the outfield talking instead of paying attention. Now if the coach threatens to pull us both out of the game, my friend would be upset, but I would be thrilled by that "punishment." Likewise, if the coach threatens to give us both a "C," then my friend wouldn't mind, but I would be terrified and start paying attention. So which is a punishment? Which is a gift? It depends on your perspective.

The "punishments" that God threatens "evil" people with are often the same as the gifts that he blesses spiritual people with. If you don't have the love of God, then nothing God can give you would ever make you happy, and if you are filled with the love of God, then that love is an inseparable part of you and nothing in the universe can take it away.

Tests That We Create for Ourselves

Natural Consequences

So far, I have presented the two kinds of tests that come from God—tests we experience as opportunities and tests we experience as punishment. But not all tests come from God. There are two additional kinds of tests—the two that we create for ourselves. One is natural consequences, the other is tests we consciously choose.

We can't blame God for the painful natural consequences of our own free-will actions.

When Bahá'ís talk about "punishment" they often explain it in terms of natural consequences of our own actions. As we understand it, spiritual laws are just as real as natural laws. If you jump out of a window, the natural law of gravity will "punish" you with a broken leg or worse. If you lie, cheat and steal, there will be natural spiritual consequences that are also very real. We can't blame God for the painful "natural consequences" of our own free-will actions.

God alone ordereth all things and is all-powerful. Why then does He send trials to His servants?

The trials of man are of two kinds. (a) The consequences of his own actions. If a man eats too much, he ruins his digestion; if he takes poison he becomes ill or dies. If a person gambles he will lose his money; if he drinks too much he will lose his equilibrium. All these sufferings are caused by the man himself, it is quite clear therefore that certain sorrows are the result of our own deeds.

(b) Other sufferings there are, which come upon the Faithful of God. Consider the great sorrows endured by Christ and by His apostles!

Those who suffer most, attain to the greatest perfection.

'Abdu'l-Bahá

Tests that are natural consequences of our own actions are both the best and the worst. They are the best because they are completely and totally within our own power to avoid. They are the worst because it is completely and totally our responsibility to try to avoid them!

Tests can be avoided only if we are willing to examine our most entrenched habits and behaviors and make a conscious effort to change the ones that are not in harmony with our spiritual reality.

O SON OF SPIRIT! Noble have I created thee, yet thou hast abased thyself. Rise then unto that for which thou wast created.

Bahá'u'lláh

We debase ourselves when we abuse our bodies through drugs, alcohol, neglect, overeating or inactivity. We debase our spirits when we lie, cheat, steal, gamble, waste time, neglect our education, remain prejudiced, ignore God and blame others for our failures. We debase our relationships when we engage in sex without intimacy and commitment, judge others, gossip, isolate ourselves, compete rather than cooperate, rage, insult, or become violent or cruel.

These behaviors have, unfortunately, become "Standard Operating Procedure" for large segments of our culture. At the office, on TV and even in our families, we accept and even expect unhealthy behavior. Acting differently may feel odd, may alienate you from some of your friends, and may require diligent effort, but it is the only way to avoid a host of tests that are really just natural consequences.

It does little good to ask God to protect you from the consequences of these behaviors, unless you also ask God for help in changing them.

Most of us stumble through life, tripping over the consequences of our own actions without even realizing that there is an alternative to spending our lives on our knees.

How can we distinguish between tests from God and natural consequences? The truth is, we can never be 100% sure because no test is 100% one or the other. What we can do is step back from our daily actions and view our lives in light of God's purpose for us.

Most of us stumble through life, tripping over the consequences of our own actions without even realizing that there is an alternative to spending our lives on our knees. The sex addict does not realize that obsession with sex is destroying his life, the over-eater does not know what it feels like to be healthy, and the compulsive shopper does not understand that s/he is controlled by possessions. We don't realize that we are unhappy because we have never experienced spiritual joy. It is only when we slide from "quiet desperation" into the active pain of a test that we are forced to consider the impact our actions may have on our health, our relationships, and even our soul.

In our current society, where morals are considered relative and God's job is to answer prayers, not tell us how to live, it is unpopular to talk about the consequences of breaking the laws of God. But as mentioned earlier, the laws of God are just as real as the law of gravity. God does not impose them on us. God reveals them to us and helps us understand what is already true. No one says, "I don't believe in Newton, so I can ignore the law of gravity!" The law is inescapable.

Likewise, we can't say "I don't believe in my Creator, so I can create myself in a different image." God knows how we were created, and reveals guidance to help us move towards Him. When we spiritually "fall," the wise thing to do is to see if we have broken one of the universal spiritual laws that help us maintain our balance.

What is a spiritual law? A spiritual law is simply a concrete way of demonstrating a spiritual virtue in the material world. For example the spiritual law that forbids gossip is a concrete way of demonstrating the spiritual virtues of love, compassion and unity.

A spiritual law is simply a concrete way of demonstrating a spiritual virtue in the material world.

It is beyond the scope of this book to list the spiritual laws that govern human development. Many of them are already engraved upon your heart, and the rest are revealed in detail in the sacred writings of all of the world's religions. Before you do too much research into them, however, I encourage you to focus on trust, faith and forgiveness. These tools will guarantee that spiritual laws become stepping stones to growth—not stumbling blocks of fear and rebellion.

I believe that tests of natural consequence constitute the majority of the tests we face each day. For the most part, God is not blessing or punishing us with our daily tests, we are blindly torturing ourselves through our own refusal to study and follow spiritual laws. There is, however, an alternative.

The Tests We Choose

Instead of waiting around to learn from our mistakes, we can study God's spiritual laws and practice them consciously.

In preparing to write this book, I discovered that most people were aware of three kinds of tests—the gift from God, the punishment from God, and the natural consequences of our own poor choices. Very few people, however, had explored the positive implications of a fourth kind of test—those we choose ourselves.

There are two ways to choose tests. The first is to take a proactive approach. Choose a virtue or spiritual quality that you know you need more of, and find ways to practice it. This approach is especially helpful with active virtues like generosity, knowledge, reverence, kindness, etc. It is harder to plan our practice of reactive virtues like forgiveness and patience because they require outside aggravation. "Fortunately" the world usually provides enough spontaneous opportunities to practice these virtues that we don't have to arrange them in advance.

So is it "cheating" to create tests for ourselves that we know we can pass? Our puritanical side might insist on that view, but there is no reason to believe it is true. God has no desire to make us miserable. What teacher, upon hearing that a student has studied for a test will insist on making the test harder in order to guarantee failure? Of course studying for today's test will not mean we will find tomorrow's easy, and studying for a math test does not help us with our spelling. Nevertheless, preparation could make today's test so easy that it is not even perceived as test.

Most of us can remember asking family members to go through piles of flash cards for everything from math to foreign languages. By choosing to test ourselves, we can create a safe environment for both success and failure. By creating lots of small tests for ourselves, we have a better chance of succeeding when it really counts.

By choosing to test ourselves, we can create a safe environment for both success and failure.

And yes, there are times when being well-practiced in virtue really does count. For example, if you choose to practice generosity by giving regularly to a charity, then if your church burns down, or a relative is ill and needs money, you will find it easier to be of real help.

But earlier I said "no pain, no gain." Aren't tests really good for us only if they surprise or hurt us? No. They only need to stretch us. A ten-minute workout every day will strengthen our muscles, and will feel a lot better than a five-hour workout once a month! We haven't avoided our work, we have simply used personal spiritual goals to break it down into manageable steps.

The other kind of "chosen test" is one of the most wonderful and powerful tools for spiritual growth we have available to us. These tests are the ones we experience when we consciously choose to do the right thing—even when we know that there could be negative consequences for our material or emotional well-being.

These tests can be as small as telling the store clerk when you receive too much change or as large as risking your life for someone else. They can be momentary decisions or long-term commitments to the service of humanity.

There are three reasons why these tests are especially powerful. First, they are an expression of your conscious free will. Second, the consequences of your choice are not under your direct control, so they require extra faith and courage. And third, you could avoid the consequences entirely by simply making a less spiritual choice. For these reasons, your decision to follow a difficult but honorable path greatly speeds your spiritual development. The people who follow this path—from day care workers to Dr. Martin Luther King Jr.—become heroes in the eyes of the spiritually minded.

Examples of Tests We Choose

Deciding to have or adopt a child
Keeping our New Year's Resolutions
Speaking out against injustice
Responding to a call for help
Doing volunteer work
Standing up for a coworker
Choosing a career based on service, not salary
Making friends with people of another race
Making a commitment to pray every day

These and many other tests are things that many of us choose to do even though we know it will be inconvenient, time consuming or even dangerous. If we try to be aware of the virtues involved, then we will benefit even more.

Why does choosing this kind of test promote growth?

Consider the difference between going exploring and getting lost. Both give you the opportunity to wander around and learn about a new area, but one is a choice and the other is an accident. Depending on where you choose to explore, it might even be more dangerous, more difficult, and even more deadly than getting lost and praying for rescue. But exploration has a goal, it requires preparation, it relies on courage, and it brings back wisdom—even in the face of failure. Getting lost guarantees no such benefits. Choosing also means that we do not experience that "lost and out of control" feeling that can lead us to feel like victims.

There are times when the tests we give ourselves have serious and lasting consequences. For example, if you choose a career based on spiritual priorities, not income, then you will live with both the inspiration and the poverty for a long time. Contrary to popular philosophy these days, life itself is not a game. Our efforts do have an impact on our own soul and the world. That is why souls who make a conscious effort to do what is right in the face of opposition are like explorers and excellent students on the path to the knowledge of God.

Souls who make a conscious effort to do what is right in the face of opposition are like explorers on the path to the knowledge of God.

There can be no doubt whatever that, in consequence of the efforts which every man may consciously exert and as a result of the exertion of his own spiritual faculties, this mirror can be so cleansed from the dross of earthly defilements and purged from satanic fancies as to be able to draw nigh unto the meads of eternal holiness and attain the courts of everlasting fellowship.

Bahá'u'lláh

Tests that we choose in spite of the immediate consequences are very important to members of the Bahá'í Faith. Not only are we called upon to adopt spiritual disciplines such as prayer, fasting and service, but we know that being a member of a minority religion can be difficult in and of itself.

In the country of Iran, the decision to promote the Bahá'í Teachings has cost thousands of people their education, their jobs, their homes and even their lives. These people have demonstrated conclusively the strength of their spirits.

Those who declare a wish to suffer much for Christ's sake must prove their sincerity; those who proclaim their longing to make great sacrifices can only prove their truth by their deeds. Job proved the fidelity of his love for God by being faithful through his great adversity, as well as during the prosperity of his life. The apostles of Christ who steadfastly bore all their trials and sufferings—did they not prove their faithfulness? Was not their endurance the best proof? 'Abdu'l-Bahá

If all of this talk about choosing tests sounds a little crazy or even masochistic, then consider the alternatives. We cannot move forward toward God without tests. That means that we can either walk toward them with our eyes open, trip over them blindly, remain motionless with fear or run away from them screaming. You choose.

The great thing about walking forward toward tests with our eyes open is that even when we trip over unexpected tests, WE HAVE OUR EYES OPEN! That means we can look at the test, identify it, understand it, and solve it instead of getting tangled up in it over and over again.

The Crossroads

To summarize the presentation of the different kinds of tests, we can see that tests can come from our own actions or from God. In response, we can use them to grow, or let them pull us backwards.

We can imagine the interaction of these possibilities as two lines forming a grid with you and God on the ends of one line and gifts and punishment on the other.

This gives us four kinds of tests:

Tests that God gives us that help us grow.
Tests that we create for ourselves, and that we learn from.
Tests that we create and are   unwilling to grow with.
Tests from God that we turn into punishments
    by rejecting the virtues that would solve them.

Gifts

Tests from God that helped you develop your capacities	Tests you chose because you wanted to grow
Tests that helped you recognize your true worth	Tests you created by accident but learned from
Tests that inspired you to pray	Tests you stumbled into and barely passed

God ——————————— **You**

Tests that you could have passed but you chose not to	Bad habits you refuse to change
Tests that shook you to your core... but your core didn't move	Times you chose to do what was wrong and blinded yourself to the consequences

Punishments

49

As you can see, there is a whole range of possibilities. Most tests fall somewhere around the intersection—tests that were partly from God and partly of our own creation; tests that we learned a little bit from, but not as much as we could have.

My hope is that understanding tests will help you in two important ways. First, it will help you get out of the middle so that you can squeeze all of the growth possible out of every test. Awareness can turn any test—even one you failed ten years ago—into a current success. Understanding where tests come from and what we can learn from them, gives us more control over them. It allows us to take responsibility for those things we *can* control, and leave to God those things we can't.

Second, and most important, I hope that understanding the many different sources of tests helps lessen the fear, guilt, shame, anger, resentment and sadness that often accompany our trials. When we face a difficult situation, we need to be able to think clearly and creatively. If half of our mental energy is going into resisting our shame, hiding our sadness or controlling our anger, then it is not available for seeking solutions.

If we succeed in thinking of difficulties as gifts, then we can approach them with joy and prayer. Armed with these weapons, at least half of the battle is already won!

Joy gives us wings! In times of joy our strength is more vital, our intellect keener, and our understanding less clouded. We seem better able to cope with the world and to find our sphere of usefulness. But when sadness visits us we become weak, our strength leaves us, our comprehension is dim and our intelligence veiled. The actualities of life seem to elude our grasp, the eyes of our spirits fail to discover the sacred mysteries, and we become even as dead beings.

'Abdu'l-Bahá

Identifying Our Tests

When people think of different kinds of tests, they usually put them in categories like financial tests, health tests, relationship tests, and so on. But these categories don't really tell us anything about the true nature of the test. If a test is defined as an opportunity to develop a virtue, then the external source of difficulty is just the wrapping paper, so to speak. The real gift, the real nature of the test, is the virtue that is waiting to be uncovered. No one in the world can know what that virtue is, except for the person who takes the time to wrestle with the wrapping paper and look inside.

The real gift, the real nature of the test, is the virtue that is waiting to be uncovered.

Let us consider the test of the rose bushes. From the outside, it looks like all four rose bushes were facing the same test. They all had their branches pruned. That's it. They each could have said, "Ouch!" and gone on with life exactly as they had before. But they didn't. Each one of them responded to it's experience in a very different way. By exploring their responses, we can come to understand the individual tests that each faced.

The same is true with us. Life happens. But we respond to life in an infinite variety of ways. Our responses are expressions of the virtues that we have—and the ones we lack. By exploring these responses we can uncover the essence of who we are and what we are here to learn.

So let's look at the first rose bush. What clues do we have as to the nature of her test? Well, first of all, we have her actions. She put her energy into creating roots instead of leaves. Pretty stupid. So is her problem her actions? Her intelligence? How many of us have looked at a friend who was in trouble and thought, "If they would just stop doing stupid things, they wouldn't have so many tests!" But there was something that preceded the actions, and that was her emotional response. She became angry, and that anger lead her to make a self-destructive choice.

So is her problem her anger? We have all seen people who can't seem to keep their emotions in check and end up creating all sorts of problems for themselves. Would a good dose of Prozac® solve her problems?

I think not. What is anger, really? What are emotions? Where do they come from, and what purpose do they serve?

Emotions are spiritual sensations that alert us to the perceived presence or absence of a virtue.

Emotions are spiritual sensations that alert us to the perceived presence or absence of a virtue. If we think of virtues as spiritual food, then emotions are like our sense of taste and smell. We feel positive emotions when we are surrounded by positive qualities like love, honesty, kindness, etc. We feel negative emotions when these qualities are taken away from us.

Thus, when the spirit is fed with holy virtues, then is the body joyous; if the soul falls into sin, the body is in torment!

When we find truth, constancy, fidelity, and love, we are happy; but if we meet with lying, faithlessness, and deceit, we are miserable.
'Abdu'l-Bahá

Anger is the sensation we feel when we perceive an absence of justice. If someone is unfair; if we do not receive the things we feel we deserve, then we become angry. Anger, like every other emotion, is a valuable tool and a source of insight and growth. The rose bush cannot pass her test by simply turning it off.

If virtues are spiritual food, then emotions are like our spiritual sense of taste and smell.

The key word in understanding emotions is *perception*. Just as our physical senses can be fooled, our spiritual senses can be mistaken as well. How often have we each gotten very upset over a situation, only to discover that we misinterpreted someone's actions? How quickly anger can turn into forgiveness or even embarrassment!

Some people trust their emotions, others trust their minds, but neither is better than the other. Both are dependent upon clarity and purity of perception.

But what was there for the rose bush to perceive? The gardener cut her branches. She didn't even need eyes to perceive that accurately!

By perception, I mean perception of the larger context. When we perceive injustice, we are really interpreting an act as unjust. In the physical world, an act is just an act. It wouldn't matter if the rose bush's branches were cut by the gardener or by a roving band of beavers. But emotionally, it does matter. It was not the severing of the branches, but the meaning that the rose bush placed on the event that made her angry.

Our interpretation of events is determined by our beliefs. We assign meaning based on what we believe to be true about ourselves and the world around us.

Our interpretation of events is determined by our beliefs.

So, as I said at the beginning of this book, the real test that the rose bush faced was one of faith. Her belief about the gardener shaped her interpretation of his actions. Her interpretation made her angry, and her anger caused her to make self-destructive choices.

Now, lest you think that all tests are tests of faith, remember that the fourth rose bush went through the same external experience. She passed the test of faith, and was therefore given several other interesting tests to pass—tests of self-discovery, love, growth and effort.

But it does seem clear that many tests do spiral down to a question of how we feel about the world and our place in it. Whenever we find ourselves doing something that feels really stupid, rather than only focusing on changing the behavior, it is often helpful to explore the emotions that motivate the behavior, the perceptions that stimulate the emotions, and the interpretations and beliefs that inform the perceptions.

From Chain to Spiral

Now, having given you a nice neat chain of cause and effect, I must admit that finding the source of a test is often not quite that easy. Belief is the accumulated wisdom gained from previous experience. Previous experience is shaped by our own actions, which are, in turn, motivated by our emotions, which are guided by our perceptions, which are the result of our interpretations born of our beliefs... In other words, the whole thing is a process. There is usually no single point at which we can say "OK, this is where this test began."

The fact that belief, perception, emotion and action all reinforce and feed off of each other is significant in several ways.

54

First, not having a single beginning point means that we can apply virtues anywhere along the way and still have a positive effect on our future behavior. This is why behavioral therapy, psychotherapy, cognitive therapy and spiritual transformation can *all* be useful in solving problems. Sometimes we just don't have the time or energy to explore the deep spiritual significance of our situation.

For example, the first rose bush's original test was one of faith, but by midsummer, she faced a very different test. She was dying from lack of photosynthesis. While it would be nice for her to address the crisis of faith that lead her to this situation, the immediate solution to her problem would be to decide to grow a few leaves. Expressing the virtue of growth through action would remind her of the joy of growth and blossoming. This little bit of joy might help reduce her anger and remind her that getting pruned was not the end of the world—unless she chose for it to be.

So, while changing our beliefs may be the most direct way to improve our lives, it is not the only place to start. Virtues guide every aspect of our lives, because virtues are expressions of our essence. Inserting virtue anywhere along the way will help stop and reverse a negative spiral.

While changing our beliefs may be the most direct way to improve our lives, it is not the only place to start.

Even more powerful is the realization that virtues should be inserted at *every* step along the way. We were created to reflect the virtues of God. These virtues should be reflected in our beliefs, perceptions, feelings and actions. While I do not recommend going to four therapists at once, it is important to try to integrate the insights that can be gained through spiritual, cognitive, emotional and behavioral approaches to self-discovery and growth.

Looking In, Out and Down the Spiral

Another implication of the reinforcing cycle of belief, perception, feeling and behavior, is that when you try to understand the motivation for your behavior or the meaning of your tests, you may have to look back through several layers.

As adults, most of our beliefs are not based on experiences we had recently. If I am a generally angry person, it is probably not because someone cut me off in traffic last week. Something early in my life convinced me that people were generally unfair and that I could expect to find injustice in most of my daily interactions.

Of course the very culture in which we grow up is built upon a set of beliefs—many of which do not serve us well. Even if it were possible to grow up in a perfect family, our perceptions, feelings and actions would still be influenced by the unspoken and often invisible beliefs that we absorb from our environment. It can be very difficult to recognize and overcome the tests created by a universally shared misperception.

I will tell you a brief story about how I made one of my own discoveries so that you can see how subtly our beliefs shape us. I was in the practice of saying affirmations every day. That means I would write or choose a positive phrase and repeat it several dozen times as a form of meditation. I found that many phrases, like "I am a precious soul" or "I am loving and lovable" left me feeling happy and refreshed after just a few minutes. One day I decided to use what I considered to be a very powerful affirmation: "God loves me."

As I sat quietly repeating this phrase to myself, I was surprised to notice that my energy level was dropping, and I was feeling sadder by the minute. How odd! I stopped, and switched to my standard "I am precious" and immediately felt my heart lift and my mood improve.

Not believing my own senses, I switched back to "God loves me," and paid attention as my heart slowly saddened once again. What in the world was going on?

And so I sat quietly for about 15 minutes and listened to what my heart had to say about my perceptions of God's love. After praying to God for twenty years, what did I think God really felt about me?

The picture that came to me was of a kind and tolerant God, holding His nose while he held me by the foot and repeatedly dipped me in hot soapy water! God wanted to love me, but he found me so vile, so loathsome, so downright stinky that He couldn't stand to be near me. Yes, God loved me, but I made Him sick!

No wonder saying, "God loves me" made me sad. In the back of my mind, I was finishing the sentence with "even though I am disgusting." I didn't want to torture God with my presence.

Once this unconscious belief was brought to the surface, I could see the way it colored my interpretation of everything that happened to me. My perceptions of the world kept me sad and ashamed. My sorrow and shame lead to many stupid and self-destructive choices, and these choices had created consequences that served to reinforce my negative self-image.

Where had this negative image come from? Had my mother told me I was vile? Had I done something so terrible I couldn't forgive myself for it? Or had I simply absorbed the beliefs and images that lie behind the concept of original sin? These are beliefs that permeate the art, literature and social interactions of the entire Western culture!

I had absorbed the beliefs and images that lie behind the concept of original sin.

How does one escape a test that is as ubiquitous as the air we breathe? For me, the answer was to use the positive images drawn from the Bahá'í Writings. Through prayer and meditation, reading and journaling, I was able to create a new vision of my relationship with God. Envisioning myself embraced by God, I was able to set aside the beliefs that lead to anger, fear and hopelessness, and look for the gift within each situation. Like the fourth rose, I began to trust that there must be new ways to grow.

> *"...man should know his own self and recognize that which leadeth unto loftiness or lowliness, glory or abasement, wealth or poverty."*
> —*Bahá'u'lláh*

By listening to my feelings while I said my affirmations, I learned something important about my view of the world. But you don't have to do special exercises in order for your emotions to help you understand your tests.

Listening to Emotions

Suppose you are standing in a very short grocery store line that is, nevertheless, not moving at all. You feel your anxiety level increasing, and you realize that you are being blessed with a test that you instantly label as "developing patience." But is it? Are you really impatient to be driving on to your next errand, or is there some other reason why you feel so bad? If you stop and listen to what your soul is saying to your body (that is making it so agitated) you might discover that you are really feeling out of control. Or perhaps you are feeling stupid for picking the wrong line. Or maybe you've had a bad day and you feel that this is proof that God is out to get you! It could be a million things. (These are just my favorites.)

By accurately identifying your feelings, you learn something about yourself and how you subconsciously perceive certain situations. Now is when it is appropriate to apply your conscious knowledge in order to explore your interpretations and beliefs. You can consider why it feels so dangerous to be out of control, or why you hate feeling stupid. You can remind yourself that God loves you and is not "out to get you." Once you have recognized the true nature of the test, you can work on developing the appropriate spiritual quality or increase your understanding of the spiritual principles involved. Telling yourself "just be patient" would probably not be as effective in this situation.

Bigger tests will probably require more than a thirty-second "ID check" on your feelings. The death of a loved one, recurring relationship problems, poor health, financial woes—these deserve a long-term serious assessment of your feelings and their origins.

Understanding Intense Emotions

Sometimes our feelings are completely out of proportion to the test we are experiencing in the moment. When we find ourselves experiencing intense grief, terror or rage when sadness, apprehension or irritation would be more appropriate, then there may be a deeper, or perhaps *older* lesson to learn.

When we were given tests in school, we were often advised to skip over questions we couldn't answer and then come back to them after all of the problems we understood were solved. This allows us to be much more successful than if we stopped cold at the first "stumper."

Whether we realize it or not, most of us instinctively used this same technique with real-life tests that we were not quite equipped to handle as we were growing up. At the age of seven, for example, you might have experienced tests—like the death of a pet, a hospitalization or the ridicule of classmates—that you did not have the mental, spiritual or emotional capacity to understand. You might have come to tentative conclusions, like, "The things I love always leave me," or "I am not safe in the world," that were more emotional than rational. These tests would have been stored in your memory to be looked at and reassessed when you were more mature and had the resources to deal with them.

Our memories, like our thoughts and emotions, reside in our soul.

Man has also spiritual powers: imagination, which conceives things; thought, which reflects upon realities; comprehension, which comprehends realities; memory, which retains whatever man imagines, thinks and comprehends.   'Abdu'l-Bahá

Children are not very logical, so we do not tend to organize our memories in logical categories. Most of our memories get filed—not under a neat, rational label, but under an emotional charge—like sorrow, fear or anger. When a current situation evokes a mild expression of a feeling, it can draw similar, deeper and more intense feeling-related memories to the surface.

Learning the lessons of these intense emotions requires a great deal of patience because the "reason" for them might take some time to discover. As I said, there is no neat little label telling you where the emotion came from or what it is trying to tell you. It is like the difference between reading the words "sad song in minor key" and listening to a moving violin concerto (or Country Western song if you prefer.)

You may have to "sit with" the feeling for quite a while before you can name the feeling, remember the experience and identify the belief that brings your heart pain.

My wife tells a story that illustrates this idea. She does not remember feeling sad when her grandmother died. She did not cry or have any other strong, observable reaction. A long time later, however, her pet hamster died, and she was overcome with uncontrollable tears and sorrow. Viewed in the narrow context, her response was "overreacting," immature or even irrational. From a God's-eye view, however, it was an opportunity for resolution, cleansing and closure. Though the cleansing took place then, the resolution and closure came many years later when she was able to look back and understand what had happened.

From this perspective, the "here and now" tests that you may be experiencing can truly be seen as gifts from God. They may be designed to help you remember unresolved tests from earlier this week, this year or this life. The fact that you may be feeling a certain feeling again *now*, means that your soul believes you have gained the maturity and resources you need in order to learn what you are supposed to learn.

Of course, if you choose to *not* listen to your feelings, or *not* understand what you need to learn, then this problem (and the triggered emotions) will just have to stay on your list of unfinished business until the feelings surface unexpectedly again—perhaps after an even bigger test.

Section Summary

A test is defined, not by the external event, but by our response to it. Our response often feels like the only one possible to us, but in reality it is the product of an interaction of beliefs, perceptions, emotions and actions. The more we understand these factors, the more we will be able to transform them through the application of virtues. Understanding comes from looking deeply at ourselves—our inner lives, our personal past and our cultural assumptions.

Tools for Passing Tests

A Quick Test About Tests:

Okay, I have presented some pretty heavy philosophical ideas about the nature and purpose of tests. But how can they be applied to real life? After all, the story about the rose is thought provoking, but humans face very different kinds of tests.

Below is a list of situations that some people might consider tests. For each one, ask the following series of questions:

What would my reflexive response be?
What virtue would improve the situation?
What would I probably be feeling at the moment?
What virtue would improve my attitude?
What other situations make me feel the same way?
What do they have in common?
What assumptions or interpretations caused my feelings?
Are there any virtues that could shift my perspective?
What beliefs about the world guided my interpretations?
What world-view would help me turn this test into a gift?

Remember, these are just events. You are the one who gives them meaning. This exercise will help you find patterns in the meanings you assign.

1. You get in a short line at the grocery, but you watch ten people get through the line beside yours before you get checked out.
2. You get a message on your answering machine from the IRS.
3. Your doctor says you have an ulcer.
4. You go to unroll your garden hose, and it gets tied into knots.
5. You get lost on the way to a funeral.
6. The bank says they didn't receive last month's mortgage payment.
7. A good friend hangs up on you.
8. Your new haircut looks awful.
9. Your mother has cancer.

If your first reaction to this list is to think "but *everyone* would feel *** in that situation," then something you need to realize is that everyone would *not* feel the same way in these situations. Some people would not blink an eyelash at some of these situations, while others would be devastated by every one of them. Anger, shame, sorrow, fear—there is a perspective to inspire each of these. Humor, serenity, confidence, compassion—these are equally valid responses.

Wouldn't that be nice? Wouldn't you just love to be able to face each of these situations with perfect peace and joy? Wouldn't you love to have the virtues you need to feel empowering emotions and achieve appropriate responses?

You can. All you need to do is love the virtues themselves.

> *Wouldn't you love to be able to face each of these situations with perfect peace and joy?*

Loving Virtues

When the fourth rose bush was pruned, she faced a situation as difficult as any of those on the above list. What gave her the strength to learn from her situation was the simple fact that she loved to grow. In fact, *she loved the joy of growing more than she hated the pain of being cut.*

Against all of the evidence, she knew that growing was the right thing to do. She could feel in her heart that, somehow, the gardener who had helped her to grow in the past must also be preparing her to grow in the future.

If the purpose of life is for us to develop virtues, and the purpose of tests is to help us in that process, then in order for us to pass our tests, we must want to develop virtues. It is not enough to believe in virtues, to understand the value of virtues, to be able to recognize, name, spell and categorize virtues. We must love virtues. We must love virtues more than we hate the discomfort of difficult situations.

We must love virtues more than we hate the discomfort of difficult situations.

We must love generosity more than we love money. We must love honesty more than we love comfort. We must love peace more than we love power. We must love understanding more than we love being right.

Replacing Material Attractions With Spiritual Attractions

Here is an essential point: When we want to solve a problem or change a behavior, our first inclination tends to be to try to hate, reject or attack the problem or behavior. This rarely works. The principle that "nature abhors a vacuum" applies to our lives as well. We cannot simply get rid of a bad habit, we have to replace it with something good. It is not enough to be angry or frustrated by our lack of helpful spiritual qualities, we must actually love the qualities that we lack. This means that we have to find something that we love instead of simply identifying what we hate.

If we hate being fat, for example, but we love eating, then our love will always win. It is not helpful to become disgusted by our lack of willpower or poor exercise habits. If our behavior repulses us, it will propel us directly *towards* our love of food. Love is com-

We cannot simply get rid of a bad habit, we have to replace it with something good.

forting, and love always wins. The answer is to concentrate on *loving* the strength, energy and well-being of being healthy. This love can provide a healthy balance for our love for food.

Likewise, you can't solve financial problems by concentrating on either the status and pleasures of material possessions, nor the pain and embarrassment of being poor. You have to learn to love the feeling of stability and security that comes from living within your means.

Similarly, relationship problems can't be solved by swearing off of romance. Instead, problems can be prevented or solved by focusing on the joys of spiritual conversation, the bonds of a shared vision and the intimacy of serving side by side. These can overshadow and replace the shallow thrill of romantic lust.

Spiritual conversation? Shared vision? Intimate service? Some of you are thinking—"What in the world is this guy talking about?" These are not goals that our culture talks about, and for many of us they are not things that we have any personal experience with.

How do we learn to love something we have never experienced? So how do we learn to love something we have never experienced? If life really is the self-generating cycle described earlier, in which our own beliefs limit our ability to interpret, perceive, feel and act, then how do we insert new virtues, new experiences, new perceptions into the process? If the people around us—our family, our friends, and our entire culture—value money, comfort, power and superiority, then how do we discover the beauty of generosity, peace and humility? If food, money and sex are our culture's measures of happiness, how do we fall in love with qualities such as health, contentment and spiritual intimacy? If we have never seen the positive effect these virtues have on our souls and in the world, then how can we even identify them as good?

The answer is that we have to find a source of virtues that is outside of our ordinary daily experience and beyond our cultural perspective. We need to see them in order to believe in them. But no *ordinary* human can step outside of him or herself far enough to discover and demonstrate such a radically different assortment of virtues. That is why God sends us Prophets and Teachers who can demonstrate the value of qualities that we would otherwise be blind to. Through Their words and actions, we can explore ideas and behaviors that we have never considered before.

This is a pivotal spiritual concept. Humans have a material side and a spiritual side. We can learn all about our material side by observing the material world around us, but in order to discover the secrets of our spiritual capacity, we must be given access to spiritual guidance. We know that humans raised in the wild by animals behave like animals—in spite of their greater intellectual and spiritual capacities. With only the example of animals to follow, humans would be just as much slaves to their instincts as every other material creature.

In order to discover the secrets of our spiritual capacity, we must be given access to spiritual guidance.

But if we are given even a glimpse of a spiritual reality, each and every one of us is capable of rising above our material natures and developing our spiritual virtues. We have to see it, not only to believe in it, but to even become conscious of the possibility of its existence. This is the primary role that the Prophets and Messengers of God have to play.

When we see how the ideas and behaviors of the Prophets can transform lives, then we begin to appreciate and even love spiritual qualities. We start to wish we had some of them in our own lives. We want to explore them, try them out, practice them. We develop a thirst for spiritual qualities.

Developing a Thirst for Spirituality

It takes a real effort to develop a hunger for virtues that is as strong as our desire for pleasure.

While we are all born with the ability to recognize and love the virtues of God within us, the material world around us does a very good job at distracting us from the more subtle refreshment of the spiritual world. It takes a real effort to develop a hunger for virtues that is as clear and powerful as our desire for physical pleasures. In the following quotation, 'Abdu'l-Bahá, the son of the Founder of the Bahá'í Faith, names some essential keys to acquire this "thirst for spirituality."

> *The first thing to do is to acquire a thirst for Spirituality, then Live the Life! Live the Life! Live the Life! The way to acquire this thirst is to meditate upon the future life. Study the Holy Words, read your Bible, read the Holy Books, especially study the Holy Utterances of Bahá'u'lláh; Prayer and Meditation, take much time for these two. Then will you know this Great Thirst, and then only can you begin to Live the Life!*
>
> 'Abdu'l-Bahá

In these few words, 'Abdu'l-Bahá has outlined the essential tools for passing tests and developing virtues. The quadruple admonition to *"live the life"* is simply a request for us to practice our virtues. But before we can *practice* them, He

68

insists, we must first be motivated by a desire or *thirst* for them. Then He gives us four tools for developing this thirst. It is interesting to note that while the admonition to live the life is about behavior, the tools for developing our thirst for spirituality all focus on transforming our beliefs and perceptions.

Appreciating the Afterlife

The first of the tools is to "*meditate upon the future life,*" by which He means the afterlife and the immortality of the soul. If we were to make a list of the biggest tests we face in life, at the top of most people's list would be #1. the death of a loved one and #2. the approach of one's own death. The theme of this book is that we overcome tests by developing our spirituality, so it is appropriate that we begin our search for spirituality by thinking deeply about our greatest test.

What we quickly realize is that the more faith we have in our continued existence after death, the less of a test death seems to be. In fact, for many of us, the thought of death can actually be a source of joy. But faith in the afterlife does more to help us pass tests than simply eliminate test #1 and test #2. The perspective we gain by seeing ourselves as eternal and spiritual be-

Seeing ourselves as eternal and spiritual beings helps us pass tests and develop virtues.

ings helps us pass other tests and develop virtues in at least three ways. 1) It helps us become less attached to the shallow and temporary pleasures of the physical world. 2) It increases our desire to acquire the virtues we will need in heaven. 3) It reminds us to keep our eyes on the "big picture"—which includes the eternal and the infinite.

Detachment

Physical pleasures are here and now. Spiritual pleasures require effort and insight. No wonder the world loves the one and ignores the other. But when we die, the situation will be different. The physical will be gone. All experience will be spiritual and virtues will be our primary source of joy. We know that will be true then. It could be true now.

Here is an analogy. Suppose you knew that in one year you were going to be sent to a beautiful new planet on a space ship. You couldn't take a single piece of baggage with you, but you *could* bring along anyone who sincerely loved you. How would you spend your year? What kind of qualities do you think you would need to develop in order to increase your passenger list? Would it be a good year?

When we "meditate on the future life," we are reminded to let go of our baggage and prepare for the long trip ahead of us.

When we "meditate on the future life," we are reminded to let go of our baggage and prepare for the long trip ahead of us. Here are some quotations about letting go of our attachments to this world.

O thou servant of God! Do not grieve at the afflictions and calamities that have befallen thee. All calamities and afflictions have been created for man so that he may spurn this mortal world—a world to which he is much attached. When he experienceth severe trials and hardships, then his nature will recoil and he will desire the eternal realm—a realm which is sanctified from all afflictions and calamities. Such is the case with the man who is wise. He shall never drink from a cup which is at the end distasteful, but, on the contrary, he will seek the cup of pure and limpid water. He will not taste of the honey that is mixed with poison.

'Abdu'l-Bahá

O thou handmaid aflame with the fire of God's love! Grieve thou not over the troubles and hardships of this nether world, nor be thou glad in times of ease and comfort, for both shall pass away. This present life is even as a swelling wave, or a mirage, or drifting shadows. Could ever a distorted image on the desert serve as refreshing waters? No, by the Lord of Lords! Never can reality and the mere semblance of reality be one, and wide is the difference between fancy and fact, between truth and the phantom thereof.

Know thou that the Kingdom is the real world, and this nether place is only its shadow stretching out. A shadow hath no life of its own; its existence is only a fantasy, and nothing more; it is but images reflected in water, and seeming as pictures to the eye.

"Know thou that the Kingdom is the real world, and this nether place is only its shadow stretching out."

Rely upon God. Trust in Him. Praise Him, and call Him continually to mind. He verily turneth trouble into ease, and sorrow into solace, and toil into utter peace. He verily hath dominion over all things.

If thou wouldst hearken to my words, release thyself from the fetters of whatsoever cometh to pass. Nay rather, under all conditions thank thou thy loving Lord, and yield up thine affairs unto His Will that worketh as He pleaseth. This verily is better for thee than all else, in either world.

'Abdu'l-Bahá

O SON OF BEING! If thine heart be set upon this eternal, imperishable dominion, and this ancient, everlasting life, forsake this mortal and fleeting sovereignty. Bahá'u'lláh

Desire for Virtues

Imagine yourself on the planet I said I was sending you to. Imagine that it is illumined only by ultraviolet light, which human eyes can't see, that the people living there speak in ultrasonic tones, which humans can't hear, and live in homes that are so light and fragile that humans crash through the floor when they step through the door. It is the most beautiful, loving and delicate planet in the universe, but only if you have the right eyes, ears and body to enjoy it. It is a material place, but human bodies lack the material tools to enjoy it.

This is only a metaphor. Bahá'ís don't believe that heaven is a physical place, but if we can imagine needing different physical senses to experience a physical world, we can imagine that a spiritual world might require drastically different senses and capacities from those we use when we are alive.

How will you know that heaven is beautiful if you have no spiritual vision? How will you know that heaven is beautiful if you have no spiritual vision? How will you enjoy its bounties without spiritual "hands and feet?" How will you communicate with your friends without speech or hearing?

In the spiritual realm, our virtues are our faculties. Insight, strength of will, empathy and love, these are your eyes, arms, mouth and ears in the next world. If we fail to develop them now, we will arrive in the next world blind to its beauty, unable to move forward, and unable to communicate effectively with the souls around us.

In the following passage, 'Abdu'l-Bahá explains some of the virtues that are needed and why. I don't know about you, but it certainly makes me want to work on some virtues before I die.

Therefore, in this world he must prepare himself for the life beyond. That which he needs in the world of the Kingdom [Heaven] must be obtained here. Just as he prepared himself in the world of the matrix [womb] by acquiring forces necessary in this sphere of existence, so, likewise, the indispensable forces of the divine existence must be potentially attained in this world.

What is he in need of in the Kingdom which transcends the life and limitation of this mortal sphere? That world beyond is a world of sanctity and radiance; therefore, it is necessary that in this world he should acquire these divine attributes. In that world there is need of spirituality, faith, assurance, the knowledge and love of God. These he must attain in this world so that after his ascension from the earthly to the heavenly Kingdom he shall find all that is needful in that eternal life ready for him.

That divine world is manifestly a world of lights; therefore, man has need of illumination here. That is a world of love; the love of God is essential. It is a world of perfections; virtues, or perfections, must be acquired. That world is vivified by the breaths of the Holy Spirit; in this world we must seek them. That is the Kingdom of everlasting life; it must be attained during this vanishing existence.

> **"That divine world is manifestly a world of lights; therefore, man has need of illumination here."**

By what means can man acquire these things? How shall he obtain these merciful gifts and powers? First, through the knowledge of God. Second, through the love of God. Third, through faith. Fourth, through philanthropic deeds. Fifth, through self-sacrifice. Sixth, through severance from this world. Seventh, through sanctity and holiness. Unless he acquires these forces and attains to these requirements, he will surely be deprived of the life that is eternal. But if he possesses the knowledge of God, becomes ignited through the fire of the love of God, witnesses the great and mighty signs of the Kingdom, becomes the cause of love among mankind and lives in the utmost state of sanctity and holiness, he shall surely attain to second birth, be baptized by the Holy Spirit and enjoy everlasting existence.   'Abdu'l-Bahá

Gaining Perspective

The future life is eternal. Thinking about life after death puts our current hopes and fears, joys and problems into a much larger perspective. When the perspective gets large enough, even life-shattering tests become dots on the horizon.

Consider this analogy: When a dozen friends leap out of the darkness to yell "surprise" at your birthday party, you do not curse them for the split second of fear, you thank them for the many hours of pleasure the following celebration brings. Long-term joy is worth short-term discomfort. The sixty, eighty or even one-hundred years that your body lives will seem even briefer than that fleeting moment when compared to the eternal life of your immortal soul. You know that when you are dead, you will look back on your life and be grateful for all of the lessons you learned and the qualities you developed—in spite of the pain you went through at the time.

Long-term joy is worth short-term discomfort. So why wait? If we work on developing an eternal perspective while we are alive, we can be grateful for all of the things we *will* learn by going through the tests we are experiencing *right now!*

O ye beloved of God! When the winds blow severely, rains fall fiercely, the lightning flashes, the thunder roars, the bolt descends and storms of trial become severe, grieve not; for after this storm, verily, the divine spring will arrive, the hills and fields will become verdant, the expanses of grain will joyfully wave, the earth will become covered with blossoms, the trees will be clothed with green garments and adorned with blossoms and fruits. Thus blessings become manifest in all countries. These favors are results of those storms and hurricanes.

74

The discerning man rejoiceth at the day of trials, his breast becometh dilated at the time of severe storms, his eyes become brightened when seeing the showers of rain and gusts of wind, whereby trees are uprooted; because he foreseeth the result and the end, the leaves, blossoms and fruits; while the ignorant person becometh troubled when he seeth a storm, is saddened when it raineth severely, is terrified by the thunder and trembleth at the surging of the waves which storm the shores. 'Abdu'l-Bahá

One of the most popular stories from the Bahá'í Writings illustrates this approach to tests. I think you will find it both memorable and enlightening.

There was once a lover who had sighed for long years in separation from his beloved, and wasted in the fire of remoteness. From the rule of love, his heart was empty of patience, and his body weary of his spirit; he reckoned life without her as a mockery, and time consumed him away. How many a day he found no rest in longing for her; how many a night the pain of her kept him from sleep; his body was worn to a sigh, his heart's wound had turned him to a cry of sorrow. He had given a thousand lives for one taste of the cup of her presence, but it availed him not. The doctors knew no cure for him, and companions avoided his company; yea, physicians have no medicine for one sick of love, unless the favor of the beloved one deliver him.

At last, the tree of his longing yielded the fruit of despair, and the fire of his hope fell to ashes. Then one night he could live no more, and he went out of his house and made for the marketplace. On a sudden, a watchman followed after him. He broke into a run, with the watchman following; then other watchmen came together, and barred every passage to the weary one. And the wretched one cried from his heart, and ran here and there, and moaned to himself: "Surely this watchman is Izrá'íl, my angel of death, following so fast upon me; or he is a tyrant of men, seeking to harm me." His feet carried him on, the one bleeding with the

75

arrow of love, and his heart lamented. Then he came to a garden wall, and with untold pain he scaled it, for it proved very high; and forgetting his life, he threw himself down to the garden.

And there he beheld his beloved with a lamp in her hand, searching for a ring she had lost. When the heart-surrendered lover looked on his ravishing love, he drew a great breath and raised up his hands in prayer, crying: "O God! Give Thou glory to the watchman, and riches and long life. For the watchman was Gabriel, guiding this poor one; or he was Isráfíl, bringing life to this wretched one!"

Indeed, his words were true, for he had found many a secret justice in this seeming tyranny of the watchman, and seen how many a mercy lay hid behind the veil. Out of wrath, the guard had led him who was athirst in love's desert to the sea of his loved one, and lit up the dark night of absence with the light of reunion. He had driven one who was afar, into the garden of nearness, had guided an ailing soul to the heart's physician.

Now if the lover could have looked ahead, he would have blessed the watchman at the start, and prayed on his behalf, and he would have seen that tyranny as justice; but since the end was veiled to him, he moaned and made his plaint in the beginning. Yet those who journey in the garden-land of knowledge, because they see the end in the beginning, see peace in war and friendliness in anger.

Bahá'u'lláh

Study the Holy Words

'Abdu'l-Bahá's second tool for developing a thirst for spirituality is the study of the Holy Words. Studying the Bible, the Qur'án, the Buddhist and Hindu scriptures and the Bahá'í Sacred Writings helps us to develop our thirst for spirituality in two ways—by enlightening our minds and by inspiring our hearts.

First, the mind. The majority of this book has been about the role of tests in helping us practice our virtues. But what are the virtues we are trying to develop? What do they look like? How do they respond to different situations? Where do we look for examples and guidance?

The Sacred Writings of all of the world's major religions offer wonderful insights into the world of human virtues. The Bahá'í Faith, being the most recent world religion, includes some of the clearest, most complete explanations of our spiritual potential. Here are just a few of the thousands of verses addressing the subject of virtues.

The Sacred Writings of all of the world's major religions offer wonderful insights into the world of human virtues.

The virtues and attributes pertaining unto God are all evident and manifest, and have been mentioned and described in all the heavenly Books. Among them are trustworthiness, truthfulness, purity of heart while communing with God, forbearance, resignation to whatever the Almighty hath decreed, contentment with the things His Will hath provided, patience, nay, thankfulness in the midst of tribulation, and complete reliance, in all circumstances, upon Him. These rank, according to the estimate of God, among the highest and most laudable of all acts.

Bahá'u'lláh

For you I desire spiritual distinction—that is, you must become eminent and distinguished in morals. In the love of God you must become distinguished from all else. You must become distinguished for loving humanity, for unity and accord, for love and justice. In brief, you must become distinguished in all the virtues of the human world—for faithfulness and sincerity, for justice and fidelity, for firmness and steadfastness, for philanthropic deeds and service to the human world, for love toward every human being, for unity and accord with all people, for removing prejudices and promoting international peace. Finally, you must become distinguished for heavenly illumination and for acquiring the bestowals of God. I desire this distinction for you. 'Abdu'l-Bahá

"Be generous in prosperity, and thankful in adversity. Be worthy of the trust of thy neighbor, and look upon him with a bright and friendly face."

Be generous in prosperity, and thankful in adversity. Be worthy of the trust of thy neighbor, and look upon him with a bright and friendly face. Be a treasure to the poor, an admonisher to the rich, an answerer of the cry of the needy, a preserver of the sanctity of thy pledge. Be fair in thy judgment, and guarded in thy speech. Be unjust to no man, and show all meekness to all men. Be as a lamp unto them that walk in darkness, a joy to the sorrowful, a sea for the thirsty, a haven for the distressed, an upholder and defender of the victim of oppression. Let integrity and uprightness distinguish all thine acts. Be a home for the stranger, a balm to the suffering, a tower of strength for the fugitive. Be eyes to the blind, and a guiding light unto the feet of the erring. Be an ornament to the countenance of truth, a crown to the brow of fidelity, a pillar of the temple of righteousness, a breath of life to the body of mankind, an ensign of the hosts of justice, a luminary above the horizon of virtue, a dew to the soil of the human heart, an ark on the ocean of knowledge, a sun in the heaven of bounty, a gem on the diadem of wisdom, a shining light in the firmament of thy generation, a fruit upon the tree of humility. Bahá'u'lláh

These quotations tell our minds about the nature of virtues, but they also speak to our hearts. The admonition to study the Holy Writings is given a second meaning within the context of developing our thirst for spirituality. Scriptures' ability to describe and explain virtues must be combined with its capacity to *inspire* us to develop those virtues in the first place.

Sacred Scripture is like poetry. It is God's special art form, and like all great art, it can stir up spiritual longings and thirsts far beyond anything mere prose could convey. That is why, no matter what your religion, and no matter how well you "understand" its teachings, it is imperative that you read from its Sacred Scriptures every day. Daily reading will inspire your heart, deepen your love for God and draw forth your latent virtues.

Sacred Scripture is like poetry. It is God's special art form, and like all great art, it can stir up spiritual longings.

Consider the difference between the words that I have written in this book, and the quotations I have included. Even when they say similar things, the beauty and imagery of the quotations touch the heart in a very different way. Beyond this, there is a mystical power in the Word of God that is capable of transforming hearts and souls if we are willing to open ourselves up to it on a daily basis. The words of God are like a magnet that draws our latent but inherent spiritual qualities to the surface of our heart where they can be acknowledged and exercised.

*Intone, O My servant, the verses of God that have been re-
ceived by thee, as intoned by them who have drawn nigh unto
Him, that the sweetness of thy melody may kindle thine own soul,
and attract the hearts of all men. Whoso reciteth, in the privacy
of his chamber, the verses revealed by God, the scattering angels of
the Almighty shall scatter abroad the fragrance of the words uttered by his mouth, and shall cause the heart of every righteous
man to throb. Though he may, at first, remain unaware of its
effect, yet the virtue of the grace vouchsafed unto him must needs
sooner or later exercise its influence upon his soul. Thus have the
mysteries of the Revelation of God been decreed by virtue of the
Will of Him Who is the Source of power and wisdom.*

Bahá'u'lláh

Study the Lives of the Prophets

The words of the Prophets move our hearts in one way.
The example set by the lives of the Prophets move us in yet
another. Jesus, Moses, Bahá'u'lláh, Muhammad, Buddha and
Krishna, are all perfect mirrors of the virtues of God. When
we love them, we are loving virtues in their most pure and
personal form.

For many of us, this is an easier way to be attracted to
God's virtues than reading sacred texts. That's Okay. As long
as you are attracted to the life, example and qualities of the
Prophets, then you can't help but fall in love with their virtues. If you are simply clinging to the name of the Prophet in
hopes that this will get you into heaven, then you've missed
the point.

Prayer

Prayer, the third tool, increases our thirst for spirituality. To understand how it does that, let's first look at two important aspects of prayer: prayer as communication and prayer as supplication.

As we develop our personal relationship with God, whether it is through reading the Sacred Writings or by studying the life and example of His Prophets, we will find ourselves falling more deeply in love with our Creator. In this state, we will naturally wish to communicate with Him through prayer.

If one friend feels love for another, he will wish to say so. Though he knows that the friend is aware that he loves him, he will still wish to say so....God knows the wishes of all hearts. But the impulse to pray is a natural one, springing from man's love to God.

Prayer need not be in words, but rather in thought and attitude. But if this love and this desire are lacking, it is useless to try to force them. Words without love mean nothing. If a person talks to you as an unpleasant duty, with no love or pleasure in his meeting with you, do you wish to converse with him?

'Abdu'l-Bahá

The wisdom of prayer is this: That it causeth a connection between the servant and the True One, because in that state man with all heart and soul turneth his face towards His Highness the Almighty, seeking His association and desiring His love and compassion. The greatest happiness for a lover is to converse with his beloved, and the greatest gift for a seeker is to become familiar with the object of his longing; that is why with every soul who is attracted to the Kingdom of God, his greatest hope is to find an opportunity to entreat and supplicate before his Beloved, appeal for His mercy and grace and be immersed in the ocean of His utterance, goodness and generosity.

Besides all this, prayer and fasting is the cause of awakening and mindfulness and conducive to protection and preservation from tests....

'Abdu'l-Bahá

The prayers that are simply expressions of love and gratitude are, in many ways, the most pure prayers. They already indicate a high degree of love for God's virtues, and a desire to put them into action. But usually when we think of prayer, we think of prayers in which we ask for God's help. These prayers are particularly popular when we are deep in the middle of tests and difficulties.

The following prayer is a moving example of a request for assistance that contains within it two assurances that God is willing and able to answer our prayers.

Dispel my grief by Thy bounty and Thy generosity, O God, my God, and banish mine anguish through Thy sovereignty and Thy might. Thou seest me, O my God, with my face set towards Thee at a time when sorrows have compassed me on every side. I implore Thee, O Thou Who art the Lord of all being, and overshadowest all things visible and invisible, by Thy Name whereby Thou hast subdued the hearts and the souls of men, and by the billows of the Ocean of Thy mercy and the splendors of the Day-Star of Thy bounty, to number me with them whom nothing whatsoever hath deterred from setting their faces toward Thee, O Thou Lord of all names and Maker of the heavens!

Thou beholdest, O my Lord, the things which have befallen me in Thy days. I entreat Thee, by Him Who is the Day-Spring of Thy names and the Dawning-Place of Thine attributes, to ordain for me what will enable me to arise to serve Thee and to extol Thy virtues. Thou art, verily, the Almighty, the Most Powerful, Who art wont to answer the prayers of all men!

And, finally, I beg of Thee by the light of Thy countenance to bless my affairs, and redeem my debts, and satisfy my needs. Thou art He to Whose power and to Whose dominion every tongue hath testified, and Whose majesty and Whose sovereignty every understanding heart hath acknowledged. No God is there but Thee, Who hearest and art ready to answer.

Bahá'u'lláh

So it is Okay to ask for help from God. In fact, it is absolutely essential. It establishes a relationship and a dynamic that opens us up to our own capacity for transformation. The following quotation explains the link between prayers of supplication and developing our thirst for spirituality.

Know thou, verily, it is becoming in a weak one to supplicate to the Strong One, and it behooveth a seeker of bounty to beseech the Glorious Bountiful One. When one supplicates to his Lord, turns to Him and seeks bounty from His Ocean, this supplication brings light to his heart, illumination to his sight, life to his soul and exaltation to his being.

During thy supplications to God and thy reciting, "Thy Name is my healing," consider how thine heart is cheered, thy soul delighted by the spirit of the love of God, and thy mind attracted to the Kingdom of God! By these attractions one's ability and capacity increase. When the vessel is enlarged the water increases, and when the thirst grows the bounty of the cloud becomes agreeable to the taste of man. This is the mystery of supplication and the wisdom of stating one's wants. 'Abdu'l-Bahá

So how does God answer these prayers? Most of us have heard stories about God working miracles in answer to prayer. Unexpected money, illnesses in remission, chance meetings, these are the kinds of answers that we all pray for and can't miss when they appear. But it is clear from the previous quotation that sometimes the answer to our prayers—even prayers for healing or physical assistance—comes from the inside. Instead of being rescued by a miracle, our own "ability and capacity increase," or an unwanted "bounty" suddenly "becomes agreeable."

Sometimes God answers our prayers by increasing our ability to understand or our capacity to serve. Sometimes He answers our prayers by changing what we think we want. In other words, He changes what we are thirsty for.

Meditation

We can become more open to this change by practicing 'Abdu'l-Bahá's fourth tool, the tool of meditation.

If we pray to God for assistance and then do not wait in silence for a few moments for an answer, then we are really demanding that God solve our problems without our participation. If tests are designed to help us grow, then we are not likely to grow very much if we don't take an active part in resolving our own difficulties.

Quiet contemplation offers God the opportunity to guide us to our own solutions

Quiet contemplation offers God the opportunity to guide us to our own solutions through the inspiration of the Holy Spirit.

Bahá'u'lláh says there is a sign (from God) in every phenomenon: the sign of the intellect is contemplation and the sign of contemplation is silence, because it is impossible for a man to do two things at one time—he cannot both speak and meditate.

It is an axiomatic fact that while you meditate you are speaking with your own spirit. In that state of mind you put certain questions to your spirit and the spirit answers: the light breaks forth and the reality is revealed....

Through the faculty of meditation man attains to eternal life; through it he receives the breath of the Holy Spirit—the bestowal of the Spirit is given in reflection and meditation.

The spirit of man is itself informed and strengthened during meditation; through it affairs of which man knew nothing are unfolded before his view. Through it he receives Divine inspiration, through it he receives heavenly food.

Meditation is the key for opening the doors of mysteries. In that state man abstracts himself: in that state man withdraws himself from all outside objects; in that subjective mood he is immersed in the ocean of spiritual life and can unfold the secrets of things-in-themselves. To illustrate this, think of man as endowed with two kinds of sight; when the power of insight is being used the outward power of vision does not see.

This faculty of meditation frees man from the animal nature, discerns the reality of things, puts man in touch with God.

This faculty brings forth from the invisible plane the sciences and arts. Through the meditative faculty inventions are made possible, colossal undertakings are carried out; through it governments can run smoothly. Through this faculty man enters into the very Kingdom of God....

The meditative faculty is akin to the mirror; if you put it before earthly objects it will reflect them. Therefore if the spirit of man is contemplating earthly subjects he will be informed of these.

But if you turn the mirror of your spirits heavenwards, the heavenly constellations and the rays of the Sun of Reality will be reflected in your hearts, and the virtues of the Kingdom will be obtained. 'Abdu'l-Bahá

Meditation is the tool that allows us look behind our actions and emotions to explore our beliefs and perceptions. Further meditation allows us to identify the virtues that can transform our souls.

I would like to end this section with a wonderful presentation on the five steps of prayer, attributed to the great-grandson of Bahá'u'lláh, Shoghi Effendi. It ties together much of what I have said about the relationship between faith, prayer, meditation and action.

Dynamics of Prayer

First Step:
Pray and meditate about it. Use the prayers of the Manifestations [Prophets] as they have the greatest power. Then remain in the silence of contemplation for a few minutes.

Second Step:

Arrive at a decision and hold this. This decision is usually born during the contemplation. It may seem almost impossible of accomplishment but if it seems to be an answer to a prayer or a way of solving the problem, then immediately take the next step.

Third Step:

Have determination to carry the decision through. Many fail here. The decision, budding into determination, is blighted and instead becomes a wish or a vague longing. When determination is born, immediately take the next step.

Fourth Step:

Have faith and confidence that the power will flow through you, the right way will appear, the door will open, the right thought, the right message, the right principle or the right book will be given to you. Have confidence, and the right thing will come to your need. Then, as you rise from prayer, take at once the fifth step.

Fifth Step:

Act as though it had all been answered. Then act with tireless, ceaseless energy. And as you act, you, yourself, will become a magnet, which will attract more power to your being, until you become an unobstructed channel for the Divine power to flow through you.

Many pray but do not remain for the last half of the first step. Some who meditate arrive at a decision, but fail to hold it. Few have the determination to carry the decision through, still fewer have the confidence that the right thing will come to their need. But how many remember to act as though it had all been answered? How true are these words—"Greater than the prayer is the spirit in which it is uttered" and greater than the way it is uttered is the spirit in which it is carried out.

Attributed to Shoghi Effendi

Section Summary

Since the purpose of tests is to help us develop the virtues of God that are within us, the best way to pass (or avoid) a test is to try to insert virtues into every aspect of our lives.

The best way to insert virtues into our lives is to learn to love virtues. (Loving or hating anything else is simply a distraction.) This love of virtues comes from a thirst for spirituality that can be increased by thinking about the afterlife, reading the Holy Scriptures, praying and meditating. The goal of all of this is that we be better able to put these virtues into practice in our lives.

At the end of this book is a section of prayers for assistance with tests. You may notice that these prayers also tend to mention a number of virtues. I have noticed that at different times in my life, certain words or phrases will almost literally jump off the page as I read these prayers. A word that I didn't even notice was in a prayer one day, will suddenly bring tears to my eyes the next. I believe that this is my soul's way of letting my conscious mind know what qualities and beliefs my spirit is thirsty for.

For those of you who are not big into prayer, I have an alternative tool to share with you. It is a simple, concrete list of qualities that are worth having. You can focus on developing a different one each week. You can use them to create personal affirmations, or you can simply roll the entire list through your head when you face a difficult situation.

You don't have to ponder all of them, just run through them and see which one stands out in your mind, or reaches deep into your heart. By itself or combined with prayer, I hope that this list can give your soul at least a chance to whisper in your ear. Imagine each of these virtues as a friend, and see which one of them speaks to you in times of need.

52 Virtues:

Chastity
Cleanliness
Compassion
Confidence
Cooperation
Courage
Courtesy
Curiosity
Empathy
Enthusiasm
Faith
Friendship
Generosity
Gentleness
Grace
Gratitude
Honesty
Hope
Humility
Humor
Idealism
Imagination
Integrity
Joy
Justice
Kindness

Knowledge
Love
Loyalty
Mercy
Moderation
Nobility
Obedience
Patience
Peace
Perseverance
Prayerfulness
Purity
Respect
Responsibility
Reverence
Sacrifice
Selflessness
Serenity
Service
Sincerity
Strength
Trustworthiness
Unity
Vision
Wisdom
Wonder

Why Us, Why Them?

There is only one question that is more difficult to answer than the one we began with, and that is the question of the suffering of innocent people—especially children. This is a question that has shaped the teachings of all the world's philosophies and religions, and yet the answers have left the majority of humanity in despair.

Previous religious traditions have told us that all people suffer because we are evil at heart and deserve to suffer. Western religions say that even children deserve to suffer because of original sin, while Eastern traditions say we are born with a "karmic debt" from our "past lives" that must be redeemed through suffering.

Previous traditions have told us that all people suffer because we are evil at heart and deserve to suffer.

I would like to propose a different, and, I hope, encouraging alternative to these explanations—one that reinforces both the Justice of God and the essential goodness of the human spirit.

Before I begin, however, I must ask that if you are currently in a state of grief, do not read this section. No amount of logic can make sense out of a personal tragedy when you are in the middle of it. Skip straight to "Getting angry at God." It will do you much more good.

Now, it is helpful to break the question into two parts. *How* can God allow innocent children to suffer and call Himself just? And *why* does God allow innocent children to suffer if He is capable of stopping it?

The first question is actually fairly easy to answer if you believe in an afterlife. Many religious traditions speak of a spiritual recompense for innocent victims of accidents or oppression. The Bahá'í Writings offer this example:

> As to the subject of babes and infants and weak ones who are afflicted by the hands of oppressors: This contains great wisdom and this subject is of paramount importance. In brief, for those souls there is a recompense in another world and many details are connected with this matter. For those souls that suffering is the greatest mercy of God. Verily that mercy of the Lord is far better and preferable to all the comfort of this world and the growth and development of this place of mortality.
>
> 'Abdu'l-Bahá

If this physical world is all there is, then it is true, there is no justice anywhere in the universe. But if this physical life is just a single heartbeat in an eternal spiritual life, then it is easy to see that God will be able to make up for any suffering we might have experienced here. Does that mean, however, that we should become complacent and ignore this suffering? I think not. It is our compassion and empathy that cause us to ask the second question.

It makes sense for an adult to suffer in order to learn a virtue, but if a child suffers and dies, who is learning what?

This question is much harder. Recompense is fine, but why allow the suffering in the first place? It makes sense for an adult to suffer in order to learn a virtue, but if a child suffers and dies, who is learning what? Here the answers are not quite so clear. All I can offer are a few thoughts based on some of the concepts I've already presented in this book.

I start by restating the point I made at the beginning. The purpose of life is to develop virtues. Most virtues can be defined in terms of our relationships to others. Compassion, generosity, service—these virtues cannot exist unless someone else is in need. The more severe the need, the more it cries out to be aided by virtue.

Just as it is impossible for us to develop forgiveness without someone doing us wrong, how could we possibly develop a passion for justice and a spirit of compassion unless we could look around and see the need for these virtues in the world?

Compassion, generosity, service —these virtues cannot exist unless someone else is in need.

So what I am proposing is that the universality of the grief, the intensity of the righteous anger, the hunger for justice, and the outpouring of compassion and empathy that arise when innocent people suffer, are *themselves* the very reason for the suffering. These are noble virtues. The world is in need of them, and they cannot be called into existence in any other way.

Consider the option of allowing only the guilty to suffer. Would we bother to feel compassion? Would we work fervently to end their pain? Would the atmosphere of love and unity within society increase with the knowledge that only the guilty need to worry about unexpected difficulties? Ha.

Consider the caste system of India. In a society in which all suffering is perceived as the just consequence of past sins, the poor make little effort to improve their "preordained" situation. Likewise, the rich complacently use and abuse people who they believe "deserve" to be treated like dogs.

Of course, this same perspective creeps into attitudes towards the poor in the West as well. If we believed that the poor or homeless were innocent, how could we stand to see their poverty and suffering?

And so it is important that we each have the opportunity to witness the suffering of someone we consider too good or innocent to deserve whatever pain and sadness they are experiencing. It forces us to explore the corners of our own humanity—the depth of our compassion, the heights of our righteous indignation, the width of our generosity and the breadth of our service. It connects us to others—both the sufferers and the other observers—and reinforces our oneness.

These are important lessons. They are the gifts of the innocent, and the givers are recompensed one-hundred fold by the One Giver who holds us all in the hollow of His hand.

This brings me to the last kind of test—the one that is intended not just for an individual, but for humanity as a whole.

Testing Humanity

All of the different kinds of tests that I have discussed in relation to us as individuals, also apply to humanity as a whole. God motivates and guides individuals, groups, nations and races; allows us to suffer the consequences of our disobedience; and, when necessary, allows us to suffer in unexpected and disturbing ways. In the process of guiding humanity, sometimes relatively innocent, spiritual individuals experience overwhelming and unavoidable tests. We must have faith that these events do serve a greater purpose, and that innocent victims will receive the sure and just recompense God has promised. God is infinitely loving and just, but the broad mechanisms of His justice are often hidden from our understanding.

He will never deal unjustly with any one, neither will He task a soul beyond its power. He, verily, is the Compassionate, the All-Merciful. Bahá'u'lláh

The following quotation about the Titanic disaster explores this mystery. (In 1912 'Abdu'l-Bahá was given tickets for the Titanic, but chose instead to remain on the Cedric for the last leg of His voyage to America.)

... Although such an event is indeed regrettable, we must realize that everything which happens is due to some wisdom and that nothing happens without a reason. Therein is a mystery; but whatever the reason and mystery, it was a very sad occurrence, one which brought tears to many eyes and distress to many souls. I was greatly affected by this disaster. Some of those who were lost voyaged on the Cedric with us as far as Naples and afterward sailed upon the other ship. When I think of them, I am very sad indeed. But when I consider this calamity in another aspect, I am consoled by the realization that the worlds of God are infinite; that though they were deprived of this existence, they have other opportunities in the life beyond, even as Christ has said, "In my Father's house are many mansions." They were called away from the temporary and transferred to the eternal; they abandoned this material existence and entered the portals of the spiritual world. Foregoing the pleasures and comforts of the earthly, they now partake of a joy and happiness far more abiding and real, for they have hastened to the Kingdom of God. The mercy of God is infinite, and it is our duty to remember these departed souls in our prayers and supplications that they may draw nearer and nearer to the Source itself.

....Therefore, the souls of those who have passed away from earth and completed their span of mortal pilgrimage in the Titanic disaster have hastened to a world superior to this. They have soared away from these conditions of darkness and dim vision into the realm of light. These are the only considerations which can comfort and console those whom they have left behind.

Furthermore, these events have deeper reasons. Their object and purpose is to teach man certain lessons. We are living in a day of reliance upon material conditions. Men imagine that the great size and strength of a ship, the perfection of machinery or the skill of a navigator will ensure safety, but these disasters some-times take place that men may know that God is the real Protec-tor. If it be the will of God to protect man, a little ship may escape destruction, whereas the greatest and most perfectly constructed vessel with the best and most skillful navigator may not survive a danger such as was present on the ocean. The purpose is that the people of the world may turn to God, the One Protector; that human souls may rely upon His preservation and know that He is the real safety. These events happen in order that man's faith may be increased and strengthened....

"...these disasters sometimes take place that men may know that God is the real Protector."

Let no one imagine that these words imply that man should not be thorough and careful in his undertakings. God has endowed man with intelligence so that he may safeguard and protect himself. There-fore, he must provide and surround himself with all that scientific skill can produce. He must be deliberate, thoughtful and thor-ough in his purposes, build the best ship and provide the most experienced captain; yet, withal, let him rely upon God and con-sider God as the one Keeper. If God protects, nothing can imperil man's safety; and if it be not His will to safeguard, no amount of preparation and precaution will avail. 'Abdu'l-Bahá

Getting Angry at God

Sometimes neither the most logical explanations nor the most compassionate reassurances help. Something unfair has happened, and it is God's fault, and you are angry, and there is just no way around it. That's Okay.

God is patient. God can wait. God can even love you while He waits for you to work through this thing and get to the other side. If you ask Him to, He can even help you through it. Your anger does not frighten God—it only frightens you.

Because it is frightening to be angry at God, you may be tempted to try to find a way around it. That is what one brilliant scholar did when his son died.

It was so frightening to be angry at God that he had to take God out of the picture entirely. He wrote a famous book about how you can be a good person and still have bad things happen to you.

Your anger does not frighten God —it only frightens you.

In order to forgive God for the loss of his child, he had to believe that God did not have the ability to save his son. Bad things happen, he said, because God is powerless to stop them. God is a loving spirit Who is incapable of operating in the physical world He created. This belief let God off the hook, so the father could stop being angry.

But consider this analogy: A while back, my wife explained that it was much easier to say "no" to our children when we were poor. Any time they asked us for something that we knew wasn't spiritually or physically good for them, we could tell them, "Sorry, we just can't afford it." That was an explanation that they could understand.

Now that we have a little more money, when they ask for things (like violent video games or expensive clothes) we have to explain that what they want for themselves and what we want for them are not the same. They don't like that. It is an explanation that requires maturity to understand. But they aren't mature. They want what they want, and they feel that we are terribly unjust and cruel for not giving it to them. They get *angry* with us, and sometimes scream, shout or cry. But that's Okay. We are the parents. We know that there are bigger issues involved than short-term happiness. We want them to develop spiritual priorities and are willing to endure their tantrums in order to help them grow. We will continue to love them—before, during and after their spat of anger.

It would be so much easier just to say, "We don't have the money"—to pretend to be impoverished, even though it isn't true. Likewise, when we adults don't get what *we* think is "right" and "just" in life, it is tempting to try to impoverish God—to pretend that He just doesn't have the power to get us what we want.

But it doesn't work that way. God created the universe. God can do *anything*—even raise the dead. So if it makes you angry that He doesn't do it for *you*, then go ahead—be angry. It is Okay. My toddler is angry at me a dozen times a day. It doesn't make him a bad child or me a bad parent. Likewise, our inability to understand why God allows us to suffer does not make us evil or Him uncaring. Nor does it make Him powerless. It only means that He is wise enough to let us learn on our own.

And if you are facing a loss and need to grieve, that is Okay too. Grieve as long as you need to—just don't let your grief cause you to forget the story of the rose.

Do you still remember the rose? Clipped and pruned, she did not give up her faith in a loving Gardener, but rather she looked for lessons to be learned and grew in a hundred new and unexpected ways. Well, the story continues...

After a few years, the rose became the most beautiful flower in the plant nursery, so one day the gardener came in, dug her up by the roots, and carried her away. From the perspective of the other remaining rose bush, she was dead, dead, dead. He became lonely and angry. He cursed the gardener, and considered life a mockery.

Meanwhile, transplanted to a spot by a fountain at the entrance to a sacred shrine, the beautiful rose bush sent her fragrant perfume throughout the garden, shed her velvet petals upon those hallowed grounds and uplifted the hearts of all who entered therein.

In Conclusion

"Why me" is the ultimate question. "Who, what, when, where and how" may be the questions of scientists and historians, but *why* is the question of philosophers. It seeks to comprehend the invisible realm of meaning and purpose.

"Why me" frames the question in very personal terms, linking the individual with the guiding hand of the infinite.

It is a reasonable question. It is not too much to ask, is it, to know what part we play in the great scheme of things? And so I encourage you to continue to ask.

I believe that the ability to ask "Why?" is one of the crucial differences between humans and animals. It demonstrates our ability to contemplate the abstract and the eternal. It is the question that gives birth to philosophy and religion. From this perspective, we can think of the question "why me?" as the ultimate human question—linking the individual to the infinite and the personal to a sense of purpose. Why me?

I hope you have found the answers I have offered in this book interesting and intriguing—perhaps, I pray, even helpful and comforting. I would like to end with a short summarizing quotation from Shoghi Effendi, the great-grandson of Bahá'u'lláh. The remainder of the book contains a few prayers to assist you in overcoming tests, followed by a short summary of the Bahá'í teachings for those of you who are curious.

As we suffer these misfortunes we must remember that the Prophets of God Themselves were not immune from these things which men suffer. They knew sorrow, illness and pain too. They rose above these things through Their spirits, and that is what we must try and do too, when afflicted. The troubles of this world pass, and what we have left is what we have made of our souls; so it is to this we must look—to becoming more spiritual, drawing nearer to God, no matter what our human minds and bodies go through. Shoghi Effendi

Prayers for Assistance

Thy name is my healing, O my God, and remembrance of Thee is my remedy. Nearness to Thee is my hope, and love for Thee is my companion. Thy mercy to me is my healing and my succor in both this world and the world to come. Thou, verily, art the All-Bountiful, the All-Knowing, the All-Wise.

Bahá'u'lláh

O God! Refresh and gladden my spirit. Purify my heart. Illumine my powers. I lay all my affairs in Thy hand. Thou art my Guide and my Refuge. I will no longer be sorrowful and grieved; I will be a happy and joyful being. O God! I will no longer be full of anxiety, nor will I let trouble harass me. I will not dwell on the unpleasant things of life.

O God! Thou art more friend to me than I am to myself. I dedicate myself to Thee, O Lord. 'Abdu'l-Bahá

Remove not, O Lord, the festal board that hath been spread in Thy Name, and extinguish not the burning flame that hath been kindled by Thine unquenchable fire. Withhold not from flowing that living water of Thine that murmureth with the melody of Thy glory and Thy remembrance, and deprive not Thy servants from the fragrance of Thy sweet savors breathing forth the perfume of Thy love.

Lord! Turn the distressing cares of Thy holy ones into ease, their hardship into comfort, their abasement into glory, their sorrow into blissful joy, O Thou that holdest in Thy grasp the reins of all mankind!

Thou art, verily, the One, the Single, the Mighty, the All-Knowing, the All-Wise. 'Abdu'l-Bahá

O Lord, my God and my Haven in my distress! My Shield and my Shelter in my woes! My Asylum and Refuge in time of need and in my loneliness my Companion! In my anguish my Solace, and in my solitude a loving Friend! The Remover of the pangs of my sorrows and the Pardoner of my sins!

Wholly unto Thee do I turn, fervently imploring Thee with all my heart, my mind and my tongue, to shield me from all that runs counter to Thy will in this, the cycle of Thy divine unity, and to cleanse me of all defilement that will hinder me from seeking, stainless and unsullied, the shade of the tree of Thy grace.

Have mercy, O Lord, on the feeble, make whole the sick, and quench the burning thirst.

Gladden the bosom wherein the fire of Thy love doth smolder, and set it aglow with the flame of Thy celestial love and spirit.

Robe the tabernacles of divine unity with the vesture of holiness, and set upon my head the crown of Thy favor.

Illumine my face with the radiance of the orb of Thy bounty, and graciously aid me in ministering at Thy holy threshold.

Make my heart overflow with love for Thy creatures and grant that I may become the sign of Thy mercy, the token of Thy grace, the promoter of concord amongst Thy loved ones, devoted unto Thee, uttering Thy commemoration and forgetful of self but ever mindful of what is Thine.

O God, my God! Stay not from me the gentle gales of Thy pardon and grace, and deprive me not of the wellsprings of Thine aid and favor.

'Neath the shade of Thy protecting wings let me nestle, and cast upon me the glance of Thine all-protecting eye.

Loose my tongue to laud Thy name amidst Thy people, that my voice may be raised in great assemblies and from my lips may stream the flood of Thy praise.

Thou art, in all truth, the Gracious, the Glorified, the Mighty, the Omnipotent.   'Abdu'l-Bahá

He is the Compassionate, the All-Bountiful!

O God, my God! Thou seest me, Thou knowest me; Thou art my Haven and my Refuge. None have I sought nor any will I seek save Thee; no path have I trodden nor any will I tread but the path of Thy love. In the darksome night of despair, my eye turneth expectant and full of hope to the morn of Thy boundless favor and at the hour of dawn my drooping soul is refreshed and strengthened in remembrance of Thy beauty and perfection. He whom the grace of Thy mercy aideth, though he be but a drop, shall become the boundless ocean, and the merest atom which the outpouring of Thy loving-kindness assisteth, shall shine even as the radiant star.

Shelter under Thy protection, O Thou Spirit of purity, Thou Who art the All-Bountiful Provider, this enthralled, enkindled servant of Thine. Aid him in this world of being to remain steadfast and firm in Thy love and grant that this broken-winged bird attain a refuge and shelter in Thy divine nest that abideth upon the celestial tree. ‘Abdu’l-Bahá

He is the Gracious, the All-Bountiful!

O God, my God! Thy call hath attracted me, and the voice of Thy Pen of Glory awakened me. The stream of Thy holy utterance hath enraptured me, and the wine of Thine inspiration entranced me. Thou seest me, O Lord, detached from all things but Thee, clinging to the cord of Thy bounty and craving the wonders of Thy grace. I ask Thee, by the eternal billows of Thy loving-kindness and the shining lights of Thy tender care and favor, to grant that which shall draw me nigh unto Thee and make me rich in Thy wealth. My tongue, my pen, my whole being, testify to Thy power, Thy might, Thy grace and Thy bounty, that Thou art God and there is none other God but Thee, the Powerful, the Mighty.

I bear witness at this moment, O my God, to my helplessness and Thy sovereignty, my feebleness and Thy power. I know not that which profiteth me or harmeth me; Thou art, verily, the All-Knowing, the All-Wise. Do Thou decree for me, O Lord, my God, and my Master, that which will make me feel content with Thine eternal decree and will prosper me in every world of Thine. Thou art in truth the Gracious, the Bountiful.

Lord! Turn me not away from the ocean of Thy wealth and the heaven of Thy mercy, and ordain for me the good of this world and hereafter. Verily, Thou art the Lord of the mercy-seat, enthroned in the highest; there is none other God but Thee, the One, the All-Knowing, the All-Wise.

Bahá'u'lláh

For the Departed

O my God! O Thou forgiver of sins, bestower of gifts, dispeller of afflictions!

Verily, I beseech Thee to forgive the sins of such as have abandoned the physical garment and have ascended to the spiritual world.

O my Lord! Purify them from trespasses, dispel their sorrows, and change their darkness into light. Cause them to enter the garden of happiness, cleanse them with the most pure water, and grant them to behold Thy splendors on the loftiest mount.

'Abdu'l-Bahá

About the Bahá'í Faith

Throughout this book, you have seen the names Bahá'u'lláh and 'Abdu'l-Bahá tucked under quotations or mentioned in passing, and perhaps you have wondered, "Who are these people?" Well, with all the talk about God and virtues in this book you will probably not be surprised to learn that Bahá'u'lláh (1817-1892) was the Founder of a new religion, and that 'Abdu'l-Bahá (1844-1921) was His son. What you may be surprised to hear is that after a little more than 150 years, this religion, the Bahá'í Faith, has become the most widespread religion on earth, after Christianity, and is one of the fastest growing, with over five-million members.

If this book has been helpful to you—if it has answered questions and revealed new insights for you—then you might want to consider the possibility that the inspiration for these ideas came from God.

I realize that most books do not end with an invitation to explore the claim that God has sent a new Messenger to teach humanity—but it is the very outrageousness of the claim that should make it fairly easy to confirm or reject. Do the quotations in this book seem like the ravings of a lunatic, or do they carry the same aura of authority and truth that you find in the Bible and other Holy Writings?

As I explained in the section on learning to love virtues, Bahá'ís believe that humanity needs spiritual teachers so that we have something other than our instincts or the example of the animal world to guide us. The Prophets of God teach us about our spiritual capacities and demonstrate virtues so that we can experience them and be attracted to them. They uplift civilization, and civilizations are built around them. Unfortunately, after a while, the world remembers the name of the Messenger, but forgets the message. We worship the name, but forget the example. That is why God continues to send us new teachers. If you love the message of Christ, Moses, Buddha or Muhammad and are attracted to Their virtues, then you will find the exact same message and virtues demonstrated in the life and teachings of Bahá'u'lláh.

Christians often use the "liar, lunatic, or Lord" test to prove the truth of Christ's message. They say that if a person claims to be a philosopher, then you can take what you like of his message and leave the rest. But if a person claims to be the Mouthpiece of God, then you have to place them in one of three categories. He is crazy, which should be obvious from his teachings; he is a manipulating liar, hoping for some financial or political gain, which should be obvious from the way he lives his life; or He is the representative of the Lord, and you should pledge your life to Him.

Christ's beautiful teachings and life of sacrifice prove His station as the Messiah. I invite you to put Bahá'u'lláh's life and teachings to the same test.

If the quotations seem reasonable, but you don't understand why God would want to send yet *another* messenger after sending His Son, Jesus Christ, (or Moses or Muhammad, etc.) the Bahá'ís have an explanation.

Bahá'ís take a very long view of religious history. We believe that humanity as a whole is going through a process of growth and maturation very similar to that of a single individual. For thousands of years, God has wanted to have a mature relationship with us, but we weren't ready. We were still immature, backwards, rooted in childish, black and white, concrete thinking. In this new millennium, we are finally moving toward maturity. Now, the chaos and violence of adolescence is finally giving way to organization and cooperation. Narrow, literal thinking is opening up to abstract, global visions. We are finally able to comprehend the existence of a God Who is beyond comprehension!

For this reason, God sent the world a new Teacher, Bahá'u'lláh. He is exactly like the other founders of the world's major religions—Moses, Jesus, Buddha, Krishna and Muhammad. God did not change, but we did. So, now we are ready to hear Bahá'u'lláh's message of love, understanding, cooperation, forgiveness, growth, equality and unity. Bahá'ís in every corner of the globe work together to promote the unity of the human race, elimination of prejudice, equality of women and men, peace, education and the reuniting of all the many pieces of God's unfolding religion.

For more information, call **1-800-22-UNITE**
or visit: **www.bahai.net or www.bahai.org**

Made in the USA
San Bernardino, CA
24 February 2020

64898353R00064